Digital Design with Chisel

Digital Design with Chisel

Martin Schoeberl

Copyright © 2016–2019 Martin Schoeberl

This work is licensed under a Creative Commons Attribution-ShareAlike 4.0 International License. `http://creativecommons.org/licenses/by-sa/4.0/`

Email: `martin@jopdesign.com`
Visit the source at `https://github.com/schoeberl/chisel-book`

Published 2019 by Kindle Direct Publishing, `https://kdp.amazon.com/`

Library of Congress Cataloging-in-Publication Data

Schoeberl, Martin

>Digital Design with Chisel
>Martin Schoeberl
>Includes bibliographical references.
>ISBN 9781689336031

Manufactured in the United States of America.
Typeset by Martin Schoeberl.

Contents

Preface		**ix**
1	**Introduction**	**1**
	1.1 Installing Chisel and FPGA Tools	2
	1.2 Hello World	3
	1.3 Chisel Hello World	4
	1.4 An IDE for Chisel	5
	1.5 Source Access and eBook Features	5
	1.6 Further Reading	6
	1.7 Exercise	6
2	**Basic Components**	**9**
	2.1 Signal Types and Constants	9
	2.2 Combinational Circuits	10
	2.2.1 Multiplexer	13
	2.3 Registers	14
	2.3.1 Counting	14
	2.4 Structure with Bundle and Vec	15
	2.5 Chisel Generates Hardware	17
	2.6 Exercise	18
3	**Build Process and Testing**	**19**
	3.1 Building your Project with sbt	19
	3.1.1 Source Organization	19
	3.1.2 Running sbt	21
	3.2 Testing with Chisel	22
	3.2.1 Using ScalaTest	24
	3.3 Exercises	25
	3.3.1 A Minimal Project	26
	3.3.2 A Testing Exercise	27

4 Components — 29
- 4.1 Components in Chisel are Modules — 29
- 4.2 An Arithmetic Logic Unit — 33
- 4.3 Bulk Connections — 34
- 4.4 Lightweight Components with Functions — 35

5 Combinational Building Blocks — 37
- 5.1 Combinational Circuits — 37
- 5.2 Decoder — 39
- 5.3 Encoder — 41
- 5.4 Exercise — 42

6 Sequential Building Blocks — 43
- 6.1 Registers — 43
- 6.2 Counters — 48
  - 6.2.1 Counting Up and Down — 48
  - 6.2.2 Generating Timing with Counters — 49
  - 6.2.3 The Nerd Counter — 51
- 6.3 Memory — 51
- 6.4 Exercise — 56

7 Finite-State Machines — 57
- 7.1 Basic Finite-State Machine — 57
- 7.2 Faster Output with a Mealy FSM — 61
- 7.3 Moore versus Mealy — 65
- 7.4 Exercise — 67

8 Communicating State Machines — 69
- 8.1 A Light Flasher Example — 69
- 8.2 State Machine with Datapath — 74
  - 8.2.1 Popcount Example — 74
- 8.3 Ready-Valid Interface — 77

9 Hardware Generators — 81
- 9.1 Configure with Parameters — 81
  - 9.1.1 Simple Parameters — 81
  - 9.1.2 Functions with Type Parameters — 82
  - 9.1.3 Modules with Type Parameters — 83
  - 9.1.4 Parametrize Bundles — 84

9.2	Generate Combinational Logic	85
9.3	Use Inheritance	88

10 Example Designs   93
10.1	FIFO Buffer	93
10.2	A Serial Port	96
10.3	Exercises	103
	10.3.1 Explore FIFO Variations	103
	10.3.2 The UART	104

11 Design of a Processor   105
11.1	Start with an ALU	105
11.2	Decoding Instructions	109
11.3	Assembling Instructions	111
11.4	Exercise	113

12 Contributing to Chisel   115
12.1	Setup the Development Environment	115
12.2	Testing	116
12.3	Contribute with a Pull Request	117
12.4	Exercise	117

13 Summary   119

A Chisel Projects   121

B Chisel 2   123

Bibliography   127

List of Figures

2.1	Logic for the expression (a & b) | c. The wires can be a single bit or multiple bits. The Chisel expression, and the schematics are the same. .	11
2.2	A basic 2:1 multiplexer.	13
3.1	Source tree of a Chisel project (using sbt)	20
4.1	A design consisting of a hierarchy of components.	30
4.2	An arithmetic logic unit, or ALU for short.	33
5.1	A 2-bit to 4-bit decoder.	39
5.2	A 4-bit to 2-bit encoder.	41
6.1	A D flip-flop based register.	43
6.2	A D flip-flop based register with a synchronous reset.	45
6.3	A waveform diagram for a register with a reset.	45
6.4	A D flip-flop based register with an enable signal.	46
6.5	A waveform diagram for a register with an enable signal.	46
6.6	An adder and a register result in counter.	47
6.7	A waveform diagram for the generation of a slow frequency tick.	50
6.8	A synchronous memory.	52
6.9	A synchronous memory with forwarding for a defined read-during-write behavior.	54
7.1	A finite state machine (Moore type).	57
7.2	The state diagram of an alarm FSM.	58
7.3	A rising edge detector (Mealy type FSM).	62
7.4	A Mealy type finite state machine.	62
7.5	The state diagram of the rising edge detector as Mealy FSM.	63
7.6	The state diagram of the rising edge detector as Moore FSM.	65
7.7	Mealy and a Moore FSM waveform for rising edge detection.	65
8.1	The light flasher split into a Master FSM and a Timer FSM.	70

8.2	The light flasher split into a Master FSM, a Timer FSM, and a Counter FSM.	72
8.3	A state machine with a datapath.	74
8.4	State diagram for the popcount FSM.	75
8.5	Datapath for the popcount circuit.	76
8.6	The ready-valid flow control.	77
10.1	A writer, a FIFO buffer, and a reader.	93
10.2	One byte transmitted by a UART.	96

List of Tables

2.1	Chisel defined hardware operators.	12
2.2	Chisel defined hardware functions, invoked on v.	13
5.1	Truth table for a 2 to 4 decoder.	40
5.2	Truth table for a 4 to 2 encoder.	41
7.1	State table for the alarm FSM.	60
11.1	Leros instruction set.	106

Listings

1.1	A hardware Hello World in Chisel.	4
6.1	1 KB of synchronous memory.	53
6.2	A memory with a forwarding circuit.	55
7.1	The Chisel code for the alarm FSM.	59
7.2	Rising edge detection with a Mealy FSM.	64
7.3	Rising edge detection with a Moore FSM.	66
8.1	Master FSM of the light flasher.	71
8.2	Master FSM of the double refactored light flasher.	73
8.3	The top level of the popcount circuit.	76
8.4	Datapath of the popcount circuit.	78
8.5	The FSM of the popcount circuit.	79
9.1	Reading a text file to generate a logic table.	86
9.2	Binary to binary-coded decimal conversion.	87
9.3	Tick generation with a counter.	88
9.4	A tester for different versions of the ticker.	90
9.5	Tick generation with a down counter.	91
9.6	Tick generation by counting down to -1.	91
9.7	ScalaTest specifications for the ticker tests.	92
10.1	A single stage of the bubble FIFO.	95
10.2	A FIFO is composed of an array of FIFO bubble stages.	96
10.3	A transmitter for a serial port.	98
10.4	A single-byte buffer with a ready/valid interface.	99
10.5	A transmitter with an additional buffer.	100
10.6	A receiver for a serial port.	101
10.7	Sending "Hello World!" via the serial port.	102
10.8	Echoing data on the serial port.	102

LISTINGS

11.1 The Leros ALU. 107
11.2 The Leros ALU function written in Scala. 108
11.3 The main part of the Leros assembler. 113

Preface

This book is an introduction to digital design with the focus on using the hardware construction language Chisel. Chisel brings advances from software engineering, such as object-orientated and functional languages, into digital design.

This book addresses hardware designers and software engineers. Hardware designers, with knowledge of Verilog or VHDL, can upgrade their productivity with a modern language for their next ASIC or FPGA design. Software engineers, with knowledge of object-oriented and functional programming, can leverage their knowledge to program hardware, for example, FPGA accelerators executing in the cloud.

The approach of this book is to present small to medium-sized typical hardware components to explore digital design with Chisel.

Acknowledgements

I want to thank everyone who has worked on Chisel for creating such a cool hardware construction language. Chisel is so joyful to use and therefore worth writing a book about. I am thankful to the whole Chisel community, which is so welcoming and friendly and never tired to answer questions on Chisel.

I would also like to thank my students in the last years of an advanced computer architecture course where most of them picked up Chisel for the final project. Thank you for moving out of your comfort zone and taking up the journey of learning and using a bleeding-edge hardware description language. Many of your questions have helped to shape this book.

1 Introduction

This book is an introduction to digital system design using a modern hardware construction language, Chisel[1] [2]. In this book, we focus on a higher abstraction level than usual in digital design books, to enable you to build more complex, interacting digital systems in a shorter time.

This book and Chisel are targeting two groups of developers: (1) hardware designers and (2) software programmers. Hardware designers who are fluid in VHDL or Verilog and using other languages such as Python, Java, or Tcl to generate hardware can move to a single hardware construction language where hardware generation is part of the language and Software programmers may become interested in hardware design, e.g., as future chips from Intel will include programmable hardware to speed up programs. It is perfectly fine to use Chisel as your first hardware description language.

Chisel brings advances in software engineering, such as object-orientated and functional languages, into digital design. Chisel does not only allow to express hardware at the register-transfer level but allows you to write hardware generators.

Hardware is now commonly described with a hardware description language. The time of drawing hardware components, even with CAD tools, is over. Some high-level schematics can give an overview of the system but are not intended to describe the system. The two most common hardware description languages are Verilog and VHDL. Both languages are old, contain many legacies, and have a moving line of what constructs of the language are synthesizable to hardware. Do not get me wrong: VHDL and Verilog are perfectly able to describe a hardware block that can be synthesized into an ASIC[2]. For hardware design in Chisel, Verilog serves as an intermediate language for testing and synthesis.

This book is not a general introduction to hardware design and the fundamentals of it. For an introduction of the basics in digital design, such as how to build a gate out of CMOS transistors, refer to other digital design books. However, this book intends to teach digital design at an abstraction level that is current practice to describe ASICs or designs targeting FPGA[3]s.[4] As prerequisites for this book, we assume basic

---
[1] https://chisel.eecs.berkeley.edu/
[2] https://en.wikipedia.org/wiki/Application-specific_integrated_circuit
[3] https://en.wikipedia.org/wiki/Field-programmable_gate_array
[4] As the author is more familiar with FPGAs than ASICs as target technology, some design optimizations

knowledge of Boolean algebra[5] and the binary number system[6]. Furthermore, some programming experience in any programming language is assumed. No knowledge of Verilog or VHDL is needed. Chisel can be your first programming language to describe digital hardware. As the build process in the examples is based on sbt and make basic knowledge of the command-line interface (CLI, also called terminal or Unix shell) will be helpful.

Chisel itself is not a big language. The basic constructs fit on one page[7] and can be learned within a few days. Therefore, this book is not a big book, as well. Chisel is for sure smaller than VHDL and Verilog, which carry many legacies. The power of Chisel comes from the embedding of Chisel within Scala[8], which itself in an expressive language. Chisel inherits the feature from Scala being "a language that grows on you" [12]. However, Scala is not the topic of this book. The textbook by Odersky et al. [12] provides a general introduction to Scala. This book is a tutorial in digital design and the Chisel language; it is not a Chisel language reference, nor is it a book on complete chip design.

All code examples shown in this book are extracted from complete programs that have been compiled and tested. Therefore, the code shall not contain any syntax errors. The code examples are available from the GitHub repository[9] of this book. Besides showing Chisel code, we have also tried to show useful designs and principles of good hardware description style.

This book is optimized for reading on a laptop or tablet (e.g., an iPad). We include links to further reading in the running text, mostly to Wikipedia[10] articles.

1.1 Installing Chisel and FPGA Tools

Chisel is a Scala library, and the easiest way to install Chisel and Scala is with sbt, the Scala build tool. Scala itself depends on the installation of the Java JDK 1.8[11].

On Mac OS X, with the packet manager Homebrew[12], sbt is installed with:

```
$ brew install sbt
```

shown in this book are targeting FPGA technology.
[5]https://en.wikipedia.org/wiki/Boolean_algebra
[6]https://en.wikipedia.org/wiki/Binary_number
[7]https://chisel.eecs.berkeley.edu/doc/chisel-cheatsheet3.pdf
[8]https://www.scala-lang.org/
[9]https://github.com/schoeberl/chisel-book
[10]https://en.wikipedia.org/
[11]https://www.oracle.com/technetwork/java/javase/downloads/jdk8-downloads-2133151.html
[12]https://brew.sh/

For Ubuntu, which is based on Debian, programs are usually installed from a Debian file (.deb). However, as of the time of this writing sbt is not available as a ready to install package. Therefore, the installation process is a little bit more involved:

```
echo "deb https://dl.bintray.com/sbt/debian /" | \
  sudo tee -a /etc/apt/sources.list.d/sbt.list
sudo apt-key adv --keyserver hkp://keyserver.ubuntu.com:80 \
  --recv 2EE0EA64E40A89B84B2DF73499E82A75642AC823
sudo apt-get update
sudo apt-get install sbt
```

Chisel and Scala can also be installed and used under Windows. sbt can be installed with a Windows installer, see: Installing sbt on Windows[13].

To build hardware for an FPGA, you need a synthesize tool. The two major FPGA vendors, Intel[14] and Xilinx, provide free versions of their tools that cover small to medium-sized FPGAs. Those medium-sized FPGAs are large enough to build multi-core RISC style processors. Intel provides the Quartus Prime Lite Edition[15] and Xilinx the Vivado Design Suite, WebPACK Edition[16].

1.2 Hello World

Each book on a programming language shall start with a minimal example, called the *Hello World* example. Following code is the first approach:

```
object HelloScala extends App{
  println("Hello Chisel World!")
}
```

Compiling and executing this short program with sbt

```
$ sbt "runMain HelloScala"
```

leads to the expected output of a Hello World program:

```
[info] Running HelloScala
Hello Chisel World!
```

---

[13]https://www.scala-sbt.org/1.x/docs/Installing-sbt-on-Windows.html
[14]former Altera
[15]https://www.altera.com/products/design-software/fpga-design/quartus-prime/download.html
[16]https://www.xilinx.com/products/design-tools/vivado/vivado-webpack.html

3

```
class Hello extends Module {
  val io = IO(new Bundle {
    val led = Output(UInt(1.W))
  })
  val CNT_MAX = (50000000 / 2 - 1).U;

  val cntReg = RegInit(0.U(32.W))
  val blkReg = RegInit(0.U(1.W))

  cntReg := cntReg + 1.U
  when(cntReg === CNT_MAX) {
    cntReg := 0.U
    blkReg := ~blkReg
  }
  io.led := blkReg
}
```

Listing 1.1: A hardware Hello World in Chisel

However, is this Chisel? Is this hardware generated to print a string? No, this is plain Scala code and not a representative Hello World program for a hardware design.

1.3 Chisel Hello World

What is then the equivalent of a Hello World program for a hardware design? The minimal useful and visible design? A blinking LED is the hardware (or even embedded software) version of Hello World. If a LED blinks, we are ready to solve bigger problems!

Listing 1.1 shows a blinking LED, described in Chisel. It is not important that you understand the details of this code example. We will cover those in the following chapters. Just note that the circuit is usually clocked with a high frequency, e.g., 50 MHz, and we need a counter to derive timing in the Hz range to achieve a visible blinking. In the above example, we count from 0 up to 25000000-1 and then toggle the blinking signal (blkReg := ~blkReg) and restart the counter (cntReg := 0.U). That hardware then blinks the LED at 1 Hz.

1.4 An IDE for Chisel

This book makes no assumptions about your programming environment or editor to use. Learning of the basics should be easy with just using sbt at the command line and an editor of your choice. In the tradition of other books, all commands that you shall type in a shell/terminal/CLI are preceded by a $ character, which you shall not type in. As an example, here is the Unix ls command, which lists files in the current folder:

```
$ ls
```

That said, an integrated development environment (IDE), where a compiler is running in the background, can speed up coding. As Chisel is a Scala library, all IDEs that support Scala are also good IDEs for Chisel. It is possible in Eclipse[17] and IntelliJ[18] to generate a project from the sbt project configuration in build.sbt. You can create an Eclipse project via

```
$ sbt eclipse
```

and import that project into Eclipse.[19] In IntelliJ you can create a new project from existing sources and then select from build.sbt.

1.5 Source Access and eBook Features

This book is open source and hosted at GitHub: chisel-book[20]. All Chisel code examples, shown in this book, are included in the repository. The code compiles with a recent version of Chisel, and many examples also include a test bench. We collect larger Chisel examples in the accompanying repository chisel-examples[21]. If you find an error or typo in the book, a GitHub pull request is the most convenient way to incorporate your improvement. You can also provide feedback or comments for improvements by filing an issue on GitHub or sending a plain, old school email.

This book is freely available as a PDF eBook and in classical printed form. The eBook version features links to further resources and Wikipedia[22] entries. We use Wikipedia entries for background information (e.g., binary number system) that does not directly fit into this book. We optimized the format of the eBook for reading on a tablet, such as an iPad.

---

[17] https://www.eclipse.org/
[18] https://www.jetbrains.com/help/idea/discover-intellij-idea-for-scala.html
[19] This function needs the Eclipse plugin for sbt.
[20] https://github.com/schoeberl/chisel-book
[21] https://github.com/schoeberl/chisel-examples
[22] https://www.wikipedia.org/

1.6 Further Reading

Here a list of further reading for digital design and Chisel:

- Digital Design: A Systems Approach[23], by William J. Dally and R. Curtis Harting, is a modern textbook on digital design. It is available in two versions: using Verilog or VHDL as a hardware description language.

The official Chisel documentation and further documents are available online:

- The Chisel[24] home page is the official starting point to download and learn Chisel.
- The Chisel Tutorial[25] provides a ready setup project containing small exercises with testers and solutions.
- The Chisel Wiki[26] contains a short users guide to Chisel and links to further information.
- The Chisel Testers[27] are in their repository that contains a Wiki documentation.
- The Generator Bootcamp[28] is a Chisel course focusing on hardware generators, as a Jupyter notebook
- A Chisel Style Guide[29] by Christopher Celio.

1.7 Exercise

Each chapter ends with a hands-on exercise. For the introduction exercise, we will use an FPGA board to get one LED[30] blinking. As a first step clone (or fork) the chisel-examples[31] repository from GitHub. The Hello World example is in the folder hello-world, set up as a minimal project. You can explore the Chisel code of the blinking LED in src/main/scala/Hello.scala. Compile the blinking LED with the following steps:

---

[23] http://www.cambridge.org/es/academic/subjects/engineering/circuits-and-systems/digital-design-systems-approach
[24] https://chisel.eecs.berkeley.edu/
[25] https://github.com/ucb-bar/chisel-tutorial
[26] https://github.com/freechipsproject/chisel3/wiki
[27] https://github.com/freechipsproject/chisel-testers
[28] https://github.com/ucb-bar/generator-bootcamp
[29] https://github.com/ccelio/chisel-style-guide
[30] https://en.wikipedia.org/wiki/Light-emitting_diode
[31] https://github.com/schoeberl/chisel-examples

```
$ git clone https://github.com/schoeberl/chisel-examples.git
$ cd chisel-examples/hello-world/
$ make
```

After some initial downloading of Chisel components, this will produce the Verilog file `Hello.v`. Explore this Verilog file. You will see that it contains two inputs `clock` and `reset` and one output `io_led`. When you compare this Verilog file with the Chisel module, you will notice that the Chisel module does not contain `clock` or `reset`. Those signals are implicitly generated, and in most designs, it is convenient not to need to deal with these low-level details. Chisel provides register components, and those are connected automatically to `clock` and `reset` (if needed).

The next step is to set up an FPGA project file for the synthesize tool, assign the pins, and compile[32] the Verilog code, and configure the FPGA with the resulting bitfile. We cannot provide the details of these steps. Please consult the manual of your Intel Quartus or Xilinx Vivado tool. However, the examples repository contains some ready to use Quartus projects in folder `quartus` for several popular FPGA boards (e.g., DE2-115). If the repository contains support for your board, start Quartus, open the project, compile it by pressing the *Play* button, and configure the FPGA board with the *Programmer* button and one of the LEDs should blink.

Gratulation! You managed to get your first design in Chisel running in an FPGA!

If the LED is not blinking, check the status of reset. On the DE2-115 configuration, the reset input is connected to SW0.

Now change the blinking frequency to a slower or a faster value and rerun the build process. Blinking frequencies and also blinking patterns communicate different "emotions". E.g., a slow blinking LED signals that everything is ok, a fast blinking LED signals an alarm state. Explore which frequencies express best those two different emotions.

As a more challenging extension to the exercise, generate the following blinking pattern: the LED shall be on for 200 ms every second. For this pattern, you might decouple the change of the LED blinking from the counter reset. You will need a second constant where you change the state of the `blkReg` register. What kind of emotion does this pattern produce? Is it alarming or more like a sign-of-live signal?

---

[32] The real process is more elaborated with following steps: synthesizing the logic, performing place and route, performing timing analysis, and generating a bitfile. However, for the purpose of this introduction example we simply call it "compile" your code.

2 Basic Components

In this section, we introduce the basic components for digital design: combinational circuits and flip-flops. These essential elements can be combined to build larger, more interesting circuits.

2.1 Signal Types and Constants

Chisel provides three data types to describe signals, combinational logic, and registers: Bits, UInt, and SInt. UInt and SInt extend Bits, and all three types represent a vector of bits. UInt gives this vector of bits the meaning of an unsigned integer and SInt of a signed integer.[1] Chisel uses two's complement[2] as signed integer representation. Here is the definition for different types, an 8-bit Bits, an 8-bit unsigned integer, and a 10-bit signed integer:

```
Bits(8.W)
UInt(8.W)
SInt(10.W)
```

The width of a vector of bits is defined by a Chisel width type (Width). The following expression casts the Scala integer n to a Chisel width, which is used for the definition of the Bits vector:

```
n.W
Bits(n.W)
```

Constants can be defined by using a Scala integer and converting it to a Chisel type:

```
0.U  // defines a UInt constant of 0
-3.S // defines a SInt constant of -3
```

Constants can also be defined with a width, by using the Chisel width type:

---

[1] The type Bits in the current version of Chisel is missing operations and therefore not very useful for user code.

[2] https://en.wikipedia.org/wiki/Two%27s_complement

2 Basic Components

```
8.U(4.W)  // An 4-bit constant of 8
```

If you find the notion of 8.U and 4.W a little bit funny, consider it as a variant of an integer constant with a type. This notation is similar to 8L, representing a long integer constant in C, Java, and Scala.

Chisel benefits from Scala's type inference and in many places type information can be left out. The same is also valid for bit widths. In many cases, Chisel will automatically infer the correct width. Therefore, a Chisel description of hardware is more concise and better readable than VHDL or Verilog.

For constants defined in other bases than decimal, the constant is defined in a string with a preceding h for hexadecimal (base 16), o for octal (base 8), and b for binary (base 2). The following example shows the definition of constant 255 in different bases. In this example we omit the bit width and Chisel infers the minimum width to fit the constants in, in this case 8 bits.

```
"hff".U            // hexadecimal representation of 255
"o377".U           // octal representation of 255
"b1111_1111".U    // binary representation of 255
```

The above code shows how to use an underscore to group digits in the string that represents a constant. The underscore is ignored.

To represent logic values, Chisel defines the type Bool. Bool can represent a *true* or *false* value. The following code shows the definition of type Bool and the definition of Bool constants, by converting the Scala Boolean constants true and false to Chisel Bool constants.

```
Bool()
true.B
false.B
```

2.2 Combinational Circuits

Chisel uses Boolean algebra[3] operators, as they are defined in C, Java, Scala, and several other programming languages, to described combinational circuits: & is the AND operator and | is the OR operator. Following line of code defines a circuit that combines signals a and b with *and* gates and combines the result with signal c with *or* gates.

```
val logic = (a & b) | c
```

---

[3]https://en.wikipedia.org/wiki/Boolean_algebra

2.2 COMBINATIONAL CIRCUITS

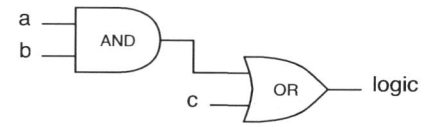

Figure 2.1: Logic for the expression (a & b) | c. The wires can be a single bit or multiple bits. The Chisel expression, and the schematics are the same.

Figure 2.1 shows the schematic of this combinatorial expression. Note that this circuit may be for a vector of bits and not only single wires that are combined with the AND and OR circuits.

In this example, we do not define the type nor the width of signal `logic`. Both are inferred from the type and width of the expression. The standard logic operations in Chisel are:

```
val and = a & b // bitwise and
val or  = a | b // bitwise or
val xor = a ^ b // bitwise xor
val not = ~a    // bitwise negation
```

The arithmetic operations use the standard operators:

```
val add = a + b // addition
val sub = a - b // subtraction
val neg = -a    // negate
val mul = a * b // multiplication
val div = a / b // division
val mod = a % b // modulo operation
```

The resulting width of the operation is the maximum width of the operators for addition and subtraction, the sum of the two widths for the multiplication, and usually the width of the numerator for divide and modulo operations.[4]

A signal can also first be defined as a `Wire` of some type. Afterward, we can assign a value to the wire with the := update operator.

```
val w = Wire(UInt())

w := a & b
```

---

[4]The exact details are available in the FIRRTL specification[5].

2 BASIC COMPONENTS

Operator	Description	Data types
* / %	multiplication, division, modulus	UInt, SInt
+ -	addition, subtraction	UInt, SInt
=== =/=	equal, not equal	UInt, SInt, returns Bool
> >= < <=	comparison	UInt, SInt, returns Bool
<< >>	shift left, shift right (sign extend on SInt)	UInt, SInt
~	NOT	UInt, SInt, Bool
& | ^	AND, OR, XOR	UInt, SInt, Bool
!	logical NOT	Bool
&& ||	logical AND, OR	Bool

Table 2.1: Chisel defined hardware operators.

A single bit can be extracted as follows:

```
val sign = x(31)
```

A subfield can be extracted from end to start position:

```
val lowByte = largeWord(7, 0)
```

Bit fields are concatenated with Cat.

```
val word = Cat(highByte, lowByte)
```

Table 2.2 shows the full list of operators (see also builtin operators[6]). The Chisel operator precedence is determined by the evaluation order of the circuit, which follows the Scala operator precedence[7]. If in doubt, it is always a good praxis to use parentheses.[8]

Table 2.2 shows various functions defined on and for Chisel data types.

---

[6] https://github.com/freechipsproject/chisel3/wiki/Builtin-Operators
[7] https://docs.scala-lang.org/tour/operators.html
[8] The operator precedence in Chisel is a side effect of the hardware elaboration when the tree of hardware nodes is created by executing the Scala operators. The Scala operator precedence is similar but not identical to Java/C. Verilog has the same operator precedence as C, but VHDL has a different one. Verilog has precedence ordering for logic operations, but in VHDL those operators have the same precedence and are evaluated from left to right.

2.2 COMBINATIONAL CIRCUITS

Function	Description	Data types
v.andR v.orR v.xorR	AND, OR, XOR reduction	UInt, SInt, returns Bool
v(n)	extraction of a single bit	UInt, SInt
v(end, start)	bitfield extraction	UInt, SInt
Fill(n, v)	bitstring replication, n times	UInt, SInt
Cat(a, b, ...)	bit field concatenation	UInt, SInt

Table 2.2: Chisel defined hardware functions, invoked on v.

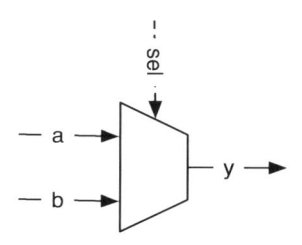

Figure 2.2: A basic 2:1 multiplexer.

2.2.1 Multiplexer

A multiplexer[9] is a circuit that selects between alternatives. In the most basic form, it selects between two alternatives. Figure 2.2 shows such a 2:1 multiplexer, or mux for short. Depending on the value of the select signal (sel) signal y will represent signal a or signal b.

A multiplexer can be built from logic. However, as multiplexing is such a standard operation, Chisel provides a multiplexer,

```
val result = Mux(sel, a, b)
```

where a is selected when the sel is true.B, otherwise b is selected. The type of sel is a Chisel Bool; the inputs a and b can be any Chisel base type or aggregate (bundles or vectors) as long as they are the same type.

With logical and arithmetical operations and a multiplexer, every combinational circuit can be described. However, Chisel provides further components and control abstractions for a more elegant description of a combinational circuit, which are described in a later chapter.

---
[9] https://en.wikipedia.org/wiki/Multiplexer

The second basic component needed to describe a digital circuit is a state element, also called register, which is described next.

2.3 Registers

Chisel provides a register, which is a collection of D flip-flops[10]. The register is implicitly connected to a global clock and is updated on the rising edge. When an initialization value is provided at the declaration of the register, it uses a synchronous reset connected to a global reset signal. A register can be any Chisel type that can be represented as a collection of bits. Following code defines an 8-bit register, initialized with 0 at reset:

```
val reg = RegInit(0.U(8.W))
```

An input is connected to the register with the := update operator and the output of the register can be used just with the name in an expression:

```
reg := d
val q = reg
```

A register can also be connected to its input at the definition:

```
val nextReg = RegNext(d)
```

A register can also be connected to its input and a constant as initial value at the definition:

```
val bothReg = RegNext(d, 0.U)
```

To distinguish between signals representing combinational logic and registers, a common practice is to postfix register names with Reg. Another common practice, coming from Java and Scala, is to use camelCase[11] for identifier consisting of several words. The convention is to start functions and variables with a lower case and classes (types) with an upper case.

2.3.1 Counting

Counting is a fundamental operation in digital systems. On might count events. However, more often counting is used to define a time interval. Counting the clock cycles and triggering an action when the time interval has expired.

---

[10]https://en.wikipedia.org/wiki/Flip-flop_(electronics)#D_flip-flop
[11]https://en.wikipedia.org/wiki/Camel_case

A simple approach is counting up to a value. However, in computer science, and digital design, counting starts at 0. Therefore, if we want to count till 10, we count from 0 to 9. The following code shows such a counter that counts till 9 and wraps around to 0 when reaching 9.

```
val cntReg = RegInit(0.U(8.W))

cntReg := Mux(cntReg === 9.U, 0.U, cntReg + 1.U)
```

2.4 Structure with Bundle and Vec

Chisel provides two constructs to group related signals: (1) a `Bundle` to group signals of different types and (2) a `Vec` to represent an indexable collection of signals of the same type. `Bundle`s and `Vec`s can be arbitrarily nested.

A Chisel bundle groups several signals. The entire bundle can be referenced as a whole, or individual fields can be accessed by their name. We can define a bundle (collection of signals) by defining a class that extends `Bundle` and list the fields as `val`s within the constructor block.

```
class Channel() extends Bundle {
  val data = UInt(32.W)
  val valid = Bool()
}
```

To use a bundle, we create it with `new` and wrap it into a `Wire`. The fields are accessed with the dot notation:

```
val ch = Wire(new Channel())
ch.data := 123.U
ch.valid := true.B

val b = ch.valid
```

Dot notation is common in object-oriented languages, where `x.y` means `x` is a reference to an object and `y` is a field of that object. As Chisel is object-oriented, we use dot notation to access fields in a bundle. A bundle is similar to a `struct` in C, a record in VHDL, or a `struct` in SystemVerilog. A bundle can also be referenced as a whole:

```
val channel = ch
```

15

A Chisel `Vec` represents a collection of signals of the same type (a vector). Each element can be accessed by an index. A Chisel `Vec` is similar to array data structures in other programing languages.[12] A `Vec` is created by calling the constructor with two parameters: the number of elements and the type of the elements. A combinational `Vec` needs to be wrapped into a `Wire`

```
val v = Wire(Vec(3, UInt(4.W)))
```

Individual elements are accessed with (index).

```
v(0) := 1.U
v(1) := 3.U
v(2) := 5.U

val idx = 1.U(2.W)
val a = v(idx)
```

A vector wrapped into a `Wire` is a multiplexer. We can also wrap a vector into a register to define an array of registers. Following example defines a register file for a processor; 32 registers each 32-bits wide, as for a classic 32-bit RISC[13] processor, like the 32-bit version of RISC-V[14].

```
val registerFile = Reg(Vec(32, UInt(32.W)))
```

An element of that register file is accessed with an index and used as a normal register.

```
registerFile(idx) := dIn
val dOut = registerFile(idx)
```

We can freely mix bundles and vectors. When creating a vector with a bundle type, we need to pass a prototype for the vector fields. Using our `Channel`, which we defined above, we can create a vector of channels with:

```
val vecBundle = Wire(Vec(8, new Channel()))
```

A bundle may as well contain a vector:

```
class BundleVec extends Bundle {
  val field = UInt(8.W)
  val vector = Vec(4,UInt(8.W))
```

---

[12]The name Array is already used in Scala.
[13]https://en.wikipedia.org/wiki/Reduced_instruction_set_computer
[14]https://en.wikipedia.org/wiki/RISC-V

}

When we want a register of a bundle type that needs a reset value, we first create a `Wire` of that bundle, set the individual fields as needed, and then passing this bundle to a RegInit:

```
val initVal = Wire(new Channel())

initVal.data  := 0.U
initVal.valid := false.B

val channelReg = RegInit(initVal)
```

With combinations of `Bundles` and `Vecs` we can define our own data structures, which are powerful abstractions.

2.5 Chisel Generates Hardware

After seeing some initial Chisel code, it might look similar to classic programming languages such as Java or C. However, Chisel (or any other hardware description language) does define hardware components. While in a software program one line of code after the other is executed, in hardware all lines of code *execute in parallel*.

It is essential to keep in mind that Chisel code does generate hardware. Try to imagine, or draw on a sheet of paper, the individual blocks that are generated by your Chisel circuit description. Each creation of a component adds hardware; each assignment statement generates gates and/or flip-flops.

More technically, when Chisel executes your code it runs as a Scala program, and by executing the Chisel statements, it *collects* the hardware components and connects those nodes. This network of hardware nodes is the hardware, which can spill out Verilog code for ASIC or FPGA synthesis or can be tested with a Chisel tester. The network of hardware nodes is what is executed in fully parallel.

For a software engineer imagine this immense parallelism that you can create in hardware without needing to partition your application into threads and getting the locking correct for the communication.

2.6 Exercise

In the introduction you implemented a blinking LED on an FPGA board (from chisel-examples[15]), which is a reasonable hardware *Hello World* example. It used only internal state, a single LED output, and no input. Copy that project into a new folder and extend it by adding some inputs to the io Bundle with val sw = Input(UInt(2.W)).

```
val io = IO(new Bundle {
  val sw = Input(UInt(2.W))
  val led = Output(UInt(1.W))
})
```

For those switches, you also need to assign the pin names for the FPGA board. You can find examples of pin assignments in the Quartus project files of the ALU project (e.g., for the DE2-115 FPGA board[16]).

When you have defined those inputs and the pin assignment, start with a simple test: drop all blinking logic from the design and connect one switch to the LED output; compile and configure the FPGA device. Can you switch the LED on an off with the switch? If yes, you have now inputs available. If not, you need to debug your FPGA configuration. The pin assignment can also be done with the GUI version of the tool.

Now use two switches and implement one of the basic combinational functions, e.g., AND two switches and show the result on the LED. Change the function. The next step involves three input switches to implement a multiplexer: one acts as a select signal, and the other two are the two inputs for the 2:1 multiplexer.

Now you have been able to implement simple combinational functions and test them in real hardware in an FPGA. As a next step, we will take a first look at how the build process works to generate an FPGA configuration. Furthermore, we will also explore a simple testing framework from Chisel, which allows you to test circuits without configuring an FPGA and toggle switches.

---

[15] https://github.com/schoeberl/chisel-examples
[16] https://github.com/schoeberl/chisel-examples/blob/master/quartus/altde2-115/alu.qsf

3 Build Process and Testing

To get started with more interesting Chisel code we first need to learn how to compile Chisel programs, how to generate Verilog code for execution in an FPGA, and how to write tests for debugging and to verify that our circuits are correct.

Chisel is written in Scala, so any build process that supports Scala is possible with a Chisel project. One popular build tool for Scala is sbt[1], which stands for the Scala interactive build tool. Besides driving the build and test process, sbt also downloads the correct version of Scala and the Chisel libraries.

3.1 Building your Project with sbt

The Scala library that represents Chisel and the Chisel testers are automatically downloaded during the build process from a Maven repository. The libraries are referenced by build.sbt. It is possible to configure build.sbt with latest.release to always use the most actual version of Chisel. However, this means on each build the version is looked up from the Maven repository. This lookup needs an Internet connection for the build to succeed. Better use a dedicated version of Chisel and all other Scala libraries in your build.sbt. Maybe sometimes it is also good to be able to write hardware code and test it without an Internet connection. For example, it is cool to do hardware design on a plane.

3.1.1 Source Organization

sbt inherits the source convention from the Maven[2] build automation tool. Maven also organizes repositories of open-source Java libraries.[3]

Figure 3.1 shows the organization of the source tree of a typical Chisel project. The root of the project is the project home, which contains build.sbt. It may also include a Makefile for the build process, a README, and a LICENSE file. Folder src contains

---
[1] https://www.scala-sbt.org/
[2] https://maven.apache.org/
[3] That is also the place where you downloaded the Chisel library on your first build: https://mvnrepository.com/artifact/edu.berkeley.cs/chisel3

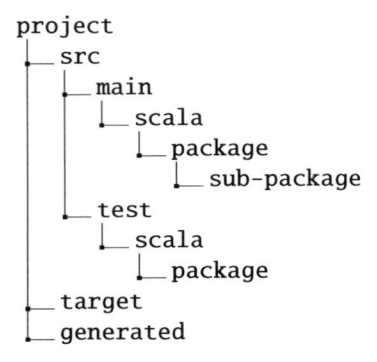

```
project
├── src
│   ├── main
│   │   └── scala
│   │       └── package
│   │           └── sub-package
│   └── test
│       └── scala
│           └── package
├── target
└── generated
```

Figure 3.1: Source tree of a Chisel project (using sbt)

all source code. From there it is split between `main`, containing the hardware sources and `test` containing testers. Chisel inherits from Scala, which inherits from Java the organization of source in packages[4]. Packages organize your Chisel code into namespaces. Packages can also contain sub-packages. The folder `target` contains the class files and other generated files. I recommend to also use a folder for generated Verilog files, which is usually call `generated`.

To use the facility of namespaces in Chisel, you need to declare that a class/module is defined in a package, in this example in `mypacket`:

```
package mypack

import chisel3._

class Abc extends Module {
  val io = IO(new Bundle{})
}
```

Note that in this example we see the import of the `chisel3` packet to use Chisel classes.

To use the module `Abc` in a different context (packet name space), the components of packet `mypacket` need to be imported. The underscore (_) acts as wildcard, meaning that all classes of `mypacket` are imported.

```
import mypack._
```

---

[4] https://en.wikipedia.org/wiki/Java_package

3.1 Building your Project with SBT

```
class AbcUser extends Module {
  val io = IO(new Bundle{})

  val abc = new Abc()
}
```

It is also possible to not import all types from mypacket, but use the fully qualified name mypack.Abc to refer to the module Abc in packet mypack.

```
class AbcUser2 extends Module {
  val io = IO(new Bundle{})

  val abc = new mypack.Abc()
}
```

It is also possible to import just a single class and create an instance of it:

```
import mypack.Abc

class AbcUser3 extends Module {
  val io = IO(new Bundle{})

  val abc = new Abc()
}
```

3.1.2 Running sbt

A Chisel project can be compiled and executed with a simple sbt command:

`$ sbt run`

This command will compile all your Chisel code from the source tree and searches for classes that contain an object that includes a main method, or simpler that extends App. If there is more than one such object, all objects are listed and one can be selected. You can also directly specify the object that shall be executed as a parameter to sbt:

`$ sbt "runMain mypacket.MyObject"`

Per default sbt searches only the main part of the source tree and not the test part.[5]

---

[5]This is a convention form Java/Scala that the test folder contains unit tests and not objects with a main.

3 BUILD PROCESS AND TESTING

However, Chisel testers, as described here, contain a `main`, but shall be placed in the test part of the source tree. To execute a `main` in the tester tree use following sbt command:

```
$ sbt "test:runMain mypacket.MyTester"
```

Now that we know the basic structure of a Chisel project and how to compile and run it with sbt, we can continue with a simple testing framework.

3.2 Testing with Chisel

Tests of hardware designs are usually called test benches[6]. The test bench instantiates the design under test (DUT), drives input ports, observes output ports, and compares them with expected values.

Chisel provides test benches in the form of a `PeekPokeTester`. One strength of Chisel is that it can use the full power of Scala to write those test benches. One can, for example, code the expected functionality of the hardware in a software simulator and compare the simulation of the hardware with the software simulation. This method is very efficient when testing an implementation of a processor [6].

To use the `PeekPokeTester`, following packages need to be imported:

```
import chisel3._
import chisel3.iotesters._
```

Testing a circuit contains (at least) three components: (1) the device under test (often called DUT), (2) the testing logic, also called test bench, and (3) the tester objects that contains the `main` function to start the testing.

The following code shows our simple design under test. It contains two input ports and one output port, all with a 2-bit width. The circuit does a bit-wise AND to it returns on the output:

```
class DeviceUnderTest extends Module {
  val io = IO(new Bundle {
    val a = Input(UInt(2.W))
    val b = Input(UInt(2.W))
    val out = Output(UInt(2.W))
  })
```

---

[6]https://www.xilinx.com/support/documentation/sw_manuals/xilinx10/isehelp/ise_c_simulation_test_bench.htm

3.2 Testing with Chisel

```
    io.out := io.a & io.b
}
```

The test bench for this DUT extends PeekPokeTester and has the DUT as a parameter for the constructor:

```
class TesterSimple(dut: DeviceUnderTest) extends
    PeekPokeTester(dut) {

  poke(dut.io.a, 0.U)
  poke(dut.io.b, 1.U)
  step(1)
  println("Result is: " + peek(dut.io.out).toString)
  poke(dut.io.a, 3.U)
  poke(dut.io.b, 2.U)
  step(1)
  println("Result is: " + peek(dut.io.out).toString)
}
```

A PeekPokeTester can set input values with poke() and read back output values with peek(). The tester advances the simulation by one step (= one clock cycle) with step(1). We can print the values of the outputs with println().

The test is created and run with the following tester main:

```
object TesterSimple extends App {
  chisel3.iotesters.Driver(() => new DeviceUnderTest()) { c =>
    new TesterSimple(c)
  }
}
```

When you run the test, you will see the results printed to the terminal (besides other information):

```
[info] [0.004] SEED 1544207645120
[info] [0.008] Result is: 0
[info] [0.009] Result is: 2
test DeviceUnderTest Success: 0 tests passed in 7 cycles
taking 0.021820 seconds
[info] [0.010] RAN 2 CYCLES PASSED
```

We see that 0 AND 1 results in 0; 3 AND 2 results in 2. Besides manually inspecting printouts, which is an excellent starting point, we can also express our expectations in

3 Build Process and Testing

the test bench itself with `expect()`, having the output port and the expected value as parameters. The following example shows testing with `expect()`:

```
class Tester(dut: DeviceUnderTest) extends PeekPokeTester(dut) {
  poke(dut.io.a, 3.U)
  poke(dut.io.b, 1.U)
  step(1)
  expect(dut.io.out, 1)
  poke(dut.io.a, 2.U)
  poke(dut.io.b, 0.U)
  step(1)
  expect(dut.io.out, 0)
}
```

Executing this test does not print out any values from the hardware, but that all tests passed as all expect values are correct.

```
[info] [0.001] SEED 1544208437832
test DeviceUnderTest Success: 2 tests passed in 7 cycles
taking 0.018000 seconds
[info] [0.009] RAN 2 CYCLES PASSED
```

A failed test, when either the DUT or the test bench contains an error, produces an error message describing the difference between the expected and actual value. In the following, we changed the test bench to expect a 4, which is an error:

```
[info] [0.002] SEED 1544208642263
[info] [0.011] EXPECT AT 2    io_out got 0 expected 4 FAIL
test DeviceUnderTest Success: 1 tests passed in 7 cycles
taking 0.022101 seconds
[info] [0.012] RAN 2 CYCLES FAILED FIRST AT CYCLE 2
```

In this section, we described the basic testing facility with Chisel for simple tests. However, in Chisel, the full power of Scala is available to write testers.

3.2.1 Using ScalaTest

ScalaTest[7] is a testing tool for Scala (and Java), which we can use to run Chisel testers. To use it, include the library in your `build.sbt` with the following line:

---
[7]http://www.scalatest.org/

```
libraryDependencies += "org.scalatest" %% "scalatest" % "3.0.5" % "test"
```

Tests are usually found in src/test/scala and can be run with:

```
$ sbt test
```

A minimal test (a testing hello world) to test a Scala Integer addition:

```
import org.scalatest._

class ExampleSpec extends FlatSpec with Matchers {
  "Integers" should "add" in {
    val i = 2
    val j = 3
    i + j should be (5)
  }
}
```

Although Chisel testing is more heavyweight than unit testing of Scala programs, we can wrap a Chisel test into a ScalaTest class. For the Tester shown before this is:

```
class SimpleSpec extends FlatSpec with Matchers {
  "Tester" should "pass" in {
    chisel3.iotesters.Driver(() => new DeviceUnderTest()) { c =>
      new Tester(c)
    } should be (true)
  }
}
```

The main benefit of this exercise is to be able to run all tests with a simple sbt test (instead of a running main). You can run just a single test with sbt, as follows:

```
$ sbt "testOnly SimpleSpec"
```

3.3 Exercises

For this exercise, we will revisit the blinking LED from chisel-examples[8] and explore Chisel testing.

---
[8]https://github.com/schoeberl/chisel-examples

3.3.1 A Minimal Project

First, let us find out what a minimal Chisel project is. Explore the files in the Hello World[9] example. The `Hello.scala` is the single hardware source file. It contains the hardware description of the blinking LED (`class Hello`) and an `App` that generates the Verilog code.

Each file starts with the import of Chisel and related packages:

```
import chisel3._
```

Then follows the hardware description, as shown in Listing 1.1. To generate the Verilog description, we need an application. A Scala object that `extends App` is an application that implicitly generates the main function where the application starts. The only action of this application is to create a new `HelloWorld` object and pass it to the Chisel driver execute function. The first argument is an array of Strings, where build options can be set (e.g., the output folder). The following code will generate the Verilog file `Hello.v`.

```
object Hello extends App {
  chisel3.Driver.execute(Array[String](), () => new Hello())
}
```

Run the generation of the example manually with

```
$ sbt "runMain Hello"
```

and explore the generated `Hello.v` with an editor. The generated Verilog code may not be very readable, but we can find out some details. The file starts with a module `Hello`, which is the same name as our Chisel module. We can identify our LED port as `output io_led`. Pin names are the Chisel names with a prepended `io_`. Besides our LED pin, the module also contains `clock` and `reset` input signals. Those two signals are added automatically by Chisel.

Furthermore, we can identify the definition of our two registers `cntReg` and `blkReg`. We may also find the reset and update of those registers at the end of the module definition. Note, that Chisel generates a synchronous reset.

For sbt to be able to fetch the correct Scala compiler and the Chisel library, we need a `build.sbt`:

```
scalaVersion := "2.11.7"

resolvers ++= Seq(
```

---
[9]https://github.com/schoeberl/chisel-examples/tree/master/hello-world

```
    Resolver.sonatypeRepo("snapshots"),
    Resolver.sonatypeRepo("releases")
)

libraryDependencies += "edu.berkeley.cs" %% "chisel3" % "3.1.2"
```

Note that in this example, we have a concrete Chisel version number to avoid checking on each run for a new version (which will fail if we are not connected to the Internet, e.g., when doing hardware design during a flight). Change the build.sbt configuration to use the latest Chisel version by changing the library dependency to

```
libraryDependencies += "edu.berkeley.cs" %% "chisel3" %
    "latest.release"
```

and rerun the build with sbt. Is there a newer version of Chisel available and will it be automatically downloaded?

For convenience, the project also contains a Makefile. It just contains the sbt command, so we do not need to remember it and can generate the Verilog code with:

```
make
```

Besides a README file, the example project also contains project files for different FPGA board. E.g., in quartus/altde2-115[10] you can find the two project files to define a Quartus project for the DE2-115 board. The main definitions (source files, device, pin assignments) can be found in a plain text file hello.qsf[11]. Explore the file and find out which pins are connected to which signals. If you need to adapt the project to a different board, there is where the changes are applied. If you have Quartus installed, open that project, compile with the green *Play* button, and then configure the FPGA.

Note that the *Hello World* is a minimal Chisel project. More realistic projects have their source files organized in packages and contain testers. The next exercise will explore such a project.

3.3.2 A Testing Exercise

In the last chapter's exercise, you have extended the blinking LED example with some input to build an AND gate and a multiplexer and run this hardware in an FPGA. We will now use this example and test the functionality with a Chisel tester to automate testing

---

[10] https://github.com/schoeberl/chisel-examples/tree/master/hello-world/quartus/altde2-115

[11] https://github.com/schoeberl/chisel-examples/blob/master/hello-world/quartus/altde2-115/hello.qsf

and also to be independent of an FPGA. Use your designs from the previous chapter and add a Chisel tester to test the functionality. Try to enumerate all possible inputs and test the output with `except()`.

Testing within Chisel can speed up the debugging of your design. However, it is always a good idea to synthesize your design for an FPGA and run tests with the FPGA. There you can perform a reality check on the size of your design (usually in LUTs and flip-flops) and your performance of your design in maximum clocking frequency. As a reference point, a textbook style pipelined RISC processor may consume about 3000 4-bit LUTs and may run around 100 MHz in a low-cost FPGA (Intel Cyclone or Xilinx Spartan).

4 Components

A larger digital design is structured into a set of components, often in a hierarchical way. Each component has an interface with input and output wires, usually called ports. These are similar to input and output pins on an integrated circuit (IC). Components are connected by wiring up the inputs and outputs. Components may contain subcomponents to build the hierarchy. The outermost component, which is connected to physical pins on a chip, is called the top-level component.

Figure 4.1 shows an example design. Component C has three input ports and two output ports. The component itself is assembled out of two subcomponents: B and C, which are connected to the inputs and outputs of C. One output of A is connected to an input of B. Component D is at the same hierarchy level as component C and connected to it.

In this chapter, we will explain how components are described in Chisel and provide several examples of standard components. Those standard components serve two purposes: (1) they provide examples of Chisel code and (2) they provide a library of components ready to be reused in your design.

4.1 Components in Chisel are Modules

Hardware components are called modules in Chisel. Each module extends the class Module and contains a field io for the interface. The interface is defined by a Bundle that is wrapped into a call to IO(). The Bundle contains fields to represent input and output ports of the module. The direction is given by wrapping a field into either a call to Input() or Output(). The direction is from the view of the component itself.

The following code shows the definition of the two example components A and B from Figure 4.1:

```
class CompA extends Module {
  val io = IO(new Bundle {
    val a = Input(UInt(8.W))
    val b = Input(UInt(8.W))
    val x = Output(UInt(8.W))
    val y = Output(UInt(8.W))
```

4 Components

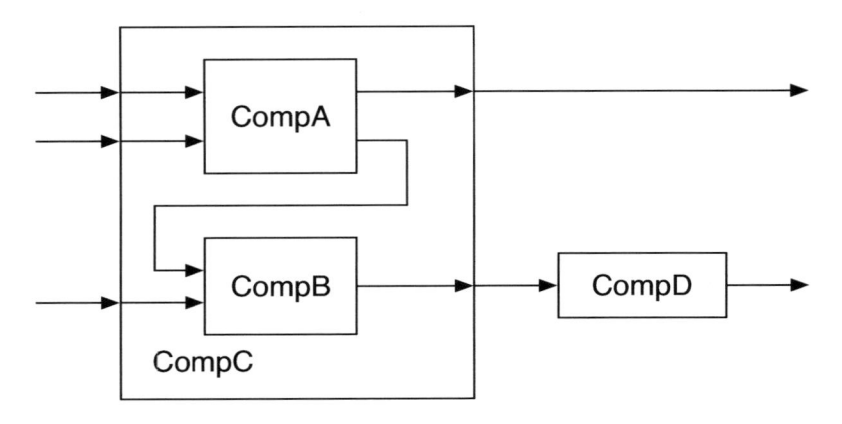

Figure 4.1: A design consisting of a hierarchy of components.

```
  })

  // function of A
}
class CompB extends Module {
  val io = IO(new Bundle {
    val in1 = Input(UInt(8.W))
    val in2 = Input(UInt(8.W))
    val out = Output(UInt(8.W))
  })

  // function of B
}
```

Component A has two inputs, named a and b, and two outputs, named x and y. For the ports of component B we chose the names in1, in2, and out. All ports use an unsigned integer (UInt) with a bit width of 8. As this example code is about connecting components and building a hierarchy, we do not show any implementation within the components. The implementation of the component is written at the place where the comments states "function of X". As we have no function associated with those example components, we used generic port names. For a real design use descriptive port names, such as data, valid, or ready.

Component C has three input and two output ports. It is built out of components A

4.1 Components in Chisel are Modules

and B. We show how A and B are connected to the ports of C and also the connection between an output port of A and an input port of B:

```
class CompC extends Module {
  val io = IO(new Bundle {
    val in_a = Input(UInt(8.W))
    val in_b = Input(UInt(8.W))
    val in_c = Input(UInt(8.W))
    val out_x = Output(UInt(8.W))
    val out_y = Output(UInt(8.W))
  })

  // create components A and B
  val compA = Module(new CompA())
  val compB = Module(new CompB())

  // connect A
  compA.io.a := io.in_a
  compA.io.b := io.in_b
  io.out_x := compA.io.x
  // connect B
  compB.io.in1 := compA.io.y
  compB.io.in2 := io.in_c
  io.out_y := compB.io.out
}
```

Components are created with new, e.g., new CompA(), and need to be wrapped into a call to Module(). The reference to that module is stored in a local variable, in this example val compA = Module(new CompA()).

With this reference, we can access the IO ports by dereferencing the io field of the module and the individual fields of the IO Bundle.

The simplest component in our design has just an input port, named in, and an output port named out.

```
class CompD extends Module {
  val io = IO(new Bundle {
    val in = Input(UInt(8.W))
    val out = Output(UInt(8.W))
  })

  // function of D
}
```

31

4 Components

The final missing piece of our example design is the top-level component, which itself is assembled out of components C and D:

```
class TopLevel extends Module {
  val io = IO(new Bundle {
    val in_a = Input(UInt(8.W))
    val in_b = Input(UInt(8.W))
    val in_c = Input(UInt(8.W))
    val out_m = Output(UInt(8.W))
    val out_n = Output(UInt(8.W))
  })

  // create C and D
  val c = Module(new CompC())
  val d = Module(new CompD())

  // connect C
  c.io.in_a := io.in_a
  c.io.in_b := io.in_b
  c.io.in_c := io.in_c
  io.out_m := c.io.out_x
  // connect D
  d.io.in := c.io.out_y
  io.out_n := d.io.out
}
```

Good component design is similar to the good design of functions or methods in software design. One of the main questions is how much functionality shall we put into a component and how large should a component be. The two extremes are tiny components, such an adder, and huge components, such as a full microprocessor,

Beginners in hardware design often start with tiny components. The problem is that digital design books use tiny components to show the principles. But the sizes of the examples (in those books, and also in this book) is small to fit into a page and to not distract by too many details.

The interface to a component is a little bit verbose (with types, names, directions, IO construction). As a rule of thumb, I would propose that the core of the component, the function, should be at least as long as the interface of the component.

For tiny components, such as a counter, Chisel provides a more lightweight way to describe them as functions that return hardware.

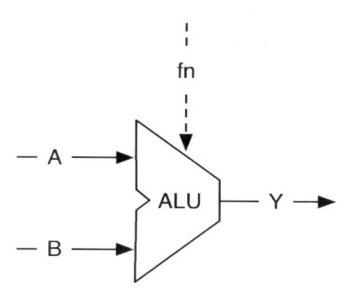

Figure 4.2: An arithmetic logic unit, or ALU for short.

4.2 An Arithmetic Logic Unit

One of the central components for circuits that compute, e.g., a microprocessor, is an arithmetic-logic unit[1], or ALU for short. Figure 4.2 shows the symbol of an ALU.

The ALU has two data inputs, labeled A and B in the figure, one function input fn, and an output, labeled Y. The ALU operates on A and B and provides the result at the output. The input fn selects the operation on A and B. The operations are usually some arithmetic, such as addition and subtraction, and some logical functions such as and, or, xor. That's why it is called ALU.

The function input fn selects the operation. The ALU is usually a combinational circuit without any state elements. An ALU might also have additional outputs to signal properties of the result, such as zero or the sign.

The following code shows an ALU with 16-bit inputs and outputs that supports: addition, subtraction, or, and and operation, selected by a 2-bit fn signal.

```
class Alu extends Module {
  val io = IO(new Bundle {
    val a  = Input(UInt(16.W))
    val b  = Input(UInt(16.W))
    val fn = Input(UInt(2.W))
    val y  = Output(UInt(16.W))
  })

  // some default value is needed
  io.y := 0.U
```

---

[1]https://en.wikipedia.org/wiki/Arithmetic_logic_unit

```
// The ALU selection
switch(io.fn) {
  is(0.U) { io.y := io.a + io.b }
  is(1.U) { io.y := io.a - io.b }
  is(2.U) { io.y := io.a | io.b }
  is(3.U) { io.y := io.a & io.b }
}
}
```

In this example, we use a new Chisel construct, the switch/is construct to describe the table that selects the output of our ALU. To use this utility function, we need to import another Chisel package:

```
import chisel3.util._
```

4.3 Bulk Connections

For connecting components with multiple IO ports, Chisel provides the bulk connection operator <>. This operator connects parts of bundles in both directions. Chisel uses the names of the leave fields for the connection. If a name is missing, it is not connected.

As an example, let us assume we build a pipelined processor. The fetch stage has a following interface:

```
class Fetch extends Module {
  val io = IO(new Bundle {
    val instr = Output(UInt(32.W))
    val pc = Output(UInt(32.W))
  })
  // ... Implementation od fetch
}
```

The next stage is the decode stage.

```
class Decode extends Module {
  val io = IO(new Bundle {
    val instr = Input(UInt(32.W))
    val pc = Input(UInt(32.W))
    val aluOp = Output(UInt(5.W))
    val regA = Output(UInt(32.W))
    val regB = Output(UInt(32.W))
  })
```

```
    // ... Implementation of decode
}
```

The final stage of our simple processor is the execute stage.

```
class Execute extends Module {
  val io = IO(new Bundle {
    val aluOp = Input(UInt(5.W))
    val regA = Input(UInt(32.W))
    val regB = Input(UInt(32.W))
    val result = Output(UInt(32.W))
  })
  // ... Implementation of execute
}
```

To connect all three stages we need just two <> operators. We can also connect the port of a submodule with the parent module.

```
val fetch = Module(new Fetch())
val decode = Module(new Decode())
val execute = Module(new Execute())

fetch.io <> decode.io
decode.io <> execute.io
io <> execute.io
```

4.4 Lightweight Components with Functions

Modules are the general way to structure your hardware description. However, there is some boilerplate code when declaring a module and when instantiating and connecting it. A lightweight way to structure your hardware is to use functions. Scala functions can take Chisel (and Scala) parameters and return generated hardware. As a simple example, we generate an adder:

```
def adder (x: UInt, y: UInt) = {
  x + y
}
```

We can then create two adders by simply calling the function adder.

```
val x = adder(a, b)
```

```
// another adder
val y = adder(c, d)
```

Note that this is a *hardware generator*. You are not executing any add operation during elaboration, but create two adders (hardware instances). The adder is an artificial example to keep it simple. Chisel has already an adder generation function, like +(that: UInt).

Functions as lightweight hardware generators can also contain state (including a register). Following example returns a one clock cycle delay element (a register). If a function has just a single statement, we can write it in one line and omit the curly braces ().

```
def delay(x: UInt) = RegNext(x)
```

By calling the function with the function itself as parameter, this generated a two clock cycle delay.

```
val delOut = delay(delay(delIn))
```

Again, this is a too short example to be useful, as `RegNext()` already is that function creating the register for the delay.

Functions can be declared as part of a `Module`. However, functions that shall be used in different modules are better placed into a Scala object that collects utility functions.

5 Combinational Building Blocks

In this chapter, we explore various combinational circuits, basic building blocks that we can use to construct more complex systems. In principle, all combinational circuits can be described with Boolean equations. However, more often, a description in the form of a table is more efficient. We let the synthesize tool extract and minimize the Boolean equations. Two basic circuits, best described in a table form, are a decoder and an encoder.

5.1 Combinational Circuits

Before describing some standard combinational building blocks, we will explore how combinational circuits can be expressed in Chisel. The simplest form is a Boolean expression, which can be assigned a name:

```
val e = (a & b) | c
```

The Boolean expression is given a name (e) by assigning it to a Scala value. The expression can be reused in other expressions:

```
val f = ~e
```

Such an expression is considered fixed. A reassignment to e with = would result in a Scala compiler error: `reassignment to val`. A try with the Chisel operator `:=`, as shown below,

```
e := c & b
```

results in a runtime exception: `Cannot reassign to read-only`.

Chisel also supports describing combinational circuits with conditional updates. Such a circuit is declared as a `Wire`. Then you uses conditional operations, such as `when`, to describe the logic of the circuit. The following code declares a `Wire` w of type `UInt` and assigns a default value of 0. The `when` block takes a Chisel `Bool` and reassigns 3 to w if cond is `true.B`.

37

5 COMBINATIONAL BUILDING BLOCKS

```
val w = Wire(UInt())

w := 0.U
when (cond) {
  w := 3.U
}
```

The logic of the circuit is a multiplexer, where the two inputs are the constants 0 and 3 and the condition cond the select signal. Keep in mind that we describe hardware circuits and not a software program with conditional execution.

The Chisel condition construct when also has a form of *else*, it is called otherwise. With assigning a value under any condition we can omit the default value assignment:

```
val w = Wire(UInt())

when (cond) {
  w := 1.U
} otherwise {
  w := 2.U
}
```

Chisel also supports a chain of conditionals (a if/elseif/else chain) with .elsewhen:

```
val w = Wire(UInt())

when (cond) {
  w := 1.U
} .elsewhen (cond2) {
  w := 2.U
} otherwise {
  w := 3.U
}
```

Note the '.' in .elsewhen that is needed to chain methods in Scala. Those .elsewhen branches can be arbitrary long. However, if the chain of conditions depends on a single signal, it is better to use the switch statement, which is introduced in the following subsection with a decoder circuit.

For more complex combinational circuits it might be practical to assign a default value to a Wire. A default assignment can be combined with the wire declaration with

38

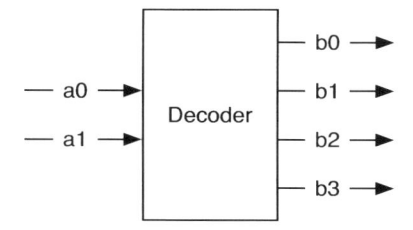

Figure 5.1: A 2-bit to 4-bit decoder.

WireDefault.[1]

```
val w = WireInit(0.U)

when (cond) {
  w := 3.U
}
// ... and some more complex conditional assignments
```

One might question why using when, .elsewhen, and otherwise when Scala has if, else if, and else? Those statements are for conditional execution of Scala code, not generating Chisel (multiplexer) hardware. Those Scala conditionals have their use in Chisel when we write circuit generators, which take parameters to conditionally generate *different* hardware instances.

5.2 Decoder

A decoder[2] converts a binary number of n bits to an m-bit signal, where $m \leq 2^n$. The output is one-hot encoded (where exactly one bit is one).

Figure 5.1 shows a 2-bit to 4-bit decoder. We can describe the function of the decoder with a truth table, such as Table 5.2.

A Chisel switch statement describes the logic as a truth table. The switch statement is not part of the core Chisel language. Therefore, we need to include the elements of the package chisel.util.

```
import chisel3.util._
```

---

[1] In the current version of Chisel it is called WireInit, but will change to WireDefault with the release of Chisel 3.2

[2] https://en.wikipedia.org/wiki/Binary_decoder

5 Combinational Building Blocks

a	b
00	0001
01	0010
10	0100
11	1000

Table 5.1: Truth table for a 2 to 4 decoder.

The following code introduces the `switch` statement of Chisel to describe a decoder:

```
result := 0.U

switch(sel) {
  is (0.U) { result := 1.U}
  is (1.U) { result := 2.U}
  is (2.U) { result := 4.U}
  is (3.U) { result := 8.U}
}
```

The above `switch` statement lists all possible values of the `sel` signal and assigns the decoded value to the `result` signal. Note that even if we enumerate all possible input values, Chisel still needs us to assign a default value, as we do by assigning 0 to `result`. This assignment will never be active and therefore optimized away by the backend tool. It is intended to avoid situations with incomplete assignments for combinational circuits (in Chisel a `Wire`) that will result in unintended latches in hardware description languages such as VHDL and Verilog. Chisel does not allow incomplete assignments.

In the example before we used unsigned integers for the signals. Maybe a clearer representation of an encode circuit uses the binary notation:

```
switch (sel) {
  is ("b00".U) { result := "b0001".U}
  is ("b01".U) { result := "b0010".U}
  is ("b10".U) { result := "b0100".U}
  is ("b11".U) { result := "b1000".U}
}
```

A table gives a very readable representation of the decoder function but is also a little bit verbose. When examining the table, we see a regular structure: a 1 is shifted left by the number represented by `sel`. Therefore, we can express a decoder with the Chisel

5.3 ENCODER

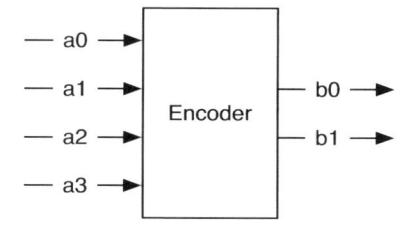

Figure 5.2: A 4-bit to 2-bit encoder.

a	b
0001	00
0010	01
0100	10
1000	11
????	??

Table 5.2: Truth table for a 4 to 2 encoder.

shift operation <<.

```
result := 1.U << sel
```

Decoders are used as a building block for a multiplexer by using the output as an enable with an AND gate for the multiplexer data input. However, in Chisel, we do not need to construct a multiplexer, as a Mux is available in the core library. Decoders can also be used for address decoding, and then the outputs are used as select signals, e.g., different IO devices connected to a microprocessor.

5.3 Encoder

An encoder[3] converts a one-hot encoded input signal into a binary encoded output signal. The encoder does the inverse operation of a decoder.

Figure 5.2 shows a 4-bit one-hot input to a 2-bit binary output encoder, and Table 5.3 shows the truth table of the encode function. However, an encoder works only as expected when the input signal is one-hot coded. For all other input values, the output is

---
[3]https://en.wikipedia.org/wiki/Encoder_(digital)

undefined. As we cannot describe a function with undefined outputs, we use a default assignment that catches all undefined input patterns.

The following Chisel code assigns a default value of 00 and then uses the switch statement for the legal input values.

```
b := "b00".U
switch (a) {
   is ("b0001".U) { b := "b00".U}
   is ("b0010".U) { b := "b01".U}
   is ("b0100".U) { b := "b10".U}
   is ("b1000".U) { b := "b11".U}
}
```

5.4 Exercise

Describe a combinational circuit to convert a 4-bit binary input to the encoding of a 7-segment display[4]. You can either define the codes for the decimal digits, which was the initial usage of a 7-segment display or additionally, define encodings for the remaining bit pattern to be able to display all 16 values of a single digit in hexadecimal[5]. When you have an FPGA board with a 7-segment display, connect 4 switches or buttons to the input of your circuit and the output to the 7-segment display.

---

[4]https://en.wikipedia.org/wiki/Seven-segment_display
[5]https://en.wikipedia.org/wiki/Hexadecimal

6 Sequential Building Blocks

Sequential circuits are circuits where the output depends on the input *and* previous values. As we are interested in synchronous design (clocked designs), we mean synchronous sequential circuits when we talk about sequential circuits.[1] To build sequential circuits, we need elements that can store state: the so-called registers.

6.1 Registers

The fundamental elements for building sequential circuits are registers. A register is a collection of D flip-flops[2]. A D flip-flop captures the value of its input at the rising edge of the clock and stores it at its output. Alternatively, in other words: the register updates its output with the value of the input on the rising edge of the clock.

Figure 6.1 shows the schematic symbol of a register. It contains an input D and an output Q. Each register also contains an input for a `clock` signal. As this global clock signal is connected to all registers in a synchronous circuit, it is usually not drawn in the schematic. The little triangle on the bottom of the box symbolizes the clock input and tells us that this is a register. We omit the clock signal in the following drawings.

---

[1] We can also build sequential circuits with asynchronous logic and feedback, but this is a specific niche topic and cannot be expressed in Chisel.

[2] https://en.wikipedia.org/wiki/Flip-flop_(electronics)#D_flip-flop

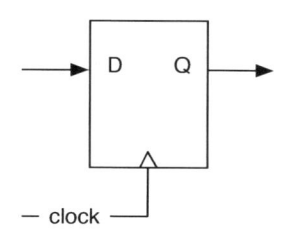

Figure 6.1: A D flip-flop based register.

6 Sequential Building Blocks

The omission of the global clock signal is also reflected by Chisel where no explicit connection of a signal to the register's clock input is needed.

In Chisel a register with input d and output q is defined with:

```
val q = RegNext(d)
```

Note that we do not need to connect a clock to the register, Chisel implicitly does this. A register's input and output can be arbitrary complex types made out of a combination of vectors and bundles.

A register can also be defined and used in two steps:

```
val delayReg = Reg(UInt(4.W))

delayReg := delayIn
```

First, we define the register and give it a name. Second, we connect the signal `delayIn` to the input of the register. Note also that the name of the register contains the string `Reg`. To easily distinguish between combinational circuits and sequential circuits, it is common practice to have the marker `Reg` as part of to the name. Also, note that names in Scala (and therefore also in Chisel) are usually in CamelCase[3]. Variable names start with lowercase and classes start with upper case.

A register can also be initialized on reset. The `reset` signal is, as the `clock` signal, implicit in Chisel. We supply the reset value, e.g., zero, as a parameter to the register constructor `RegInit`. The input for the register is connected with a Chisel assignment statement.

```
val valReg = RegInit(0.U(4.W))

valReg := inVal
```

The default implementation of reset in Chisel is a synchronous reset.[4] For a synchronous reset no change is needed on a D flip-flop, just a multiplexer needs to be added to the input that selects between the initialization value under reset and the data values.

Figure 6.2 shows the schematics of a register with a synchronous reset where the reset drives the multiplexer. However, as synchronous reset is used quite often modern FPGAs flip-flops contain a synchronous reset (and set) input to not wast LUT resources for the multiplexer.

---

[3]https://en.wikipedia.org/wiki/Camel_case
[4]Support for asynchronous reset is currently under development

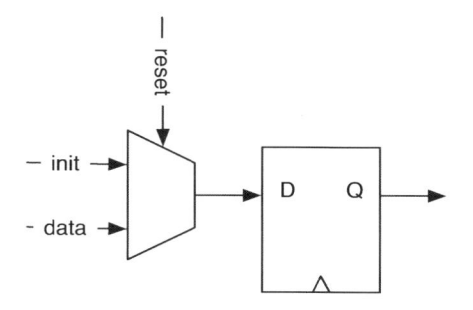

Figure 6.2: A D flip-flop based register with a synchronous reset.

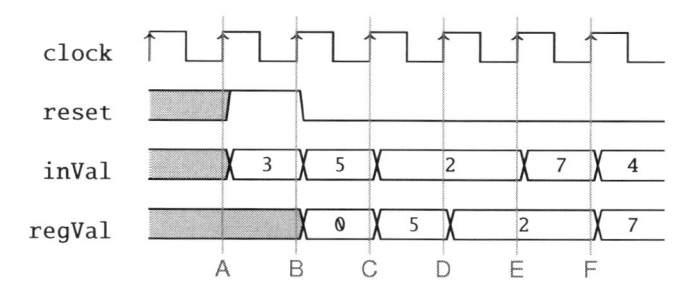

Figure 6.3: A waveform diagram for a register with a reset.

Sequential circuits change their value over time. Therefore, their behavior can be described by a diagram showing the signals over time. Such a diagram is called a waveform or timing diagram[5].

Figure 6.3 shows a waveform for the register with a reset and some input data applied to it. Time advances from left to right. On top of the figure, we see the clock that drives our circuit. In the first clock cycle, before a reset, the register is undefined. In the second clock cycle reset is asserted high, and on the rising edge of this clock cycle (labeled B) the register captures the initial value of 0. Input inVal is ignored. In the next clock cycle reset is 0, and the value of inVal is captured on the next rising edge (labeled C). From then on reset stays 0, as it should be, and the register output follows the input signal with one clock cycle delay.

Waveforms are an excellent tool to specify the behavior of a circuit graphically. Es-

---

[5]https://en.wikipedia.org/wiki/Digital_timing_diagram

6 SEQUENTIAL BUILDING BLOCKS

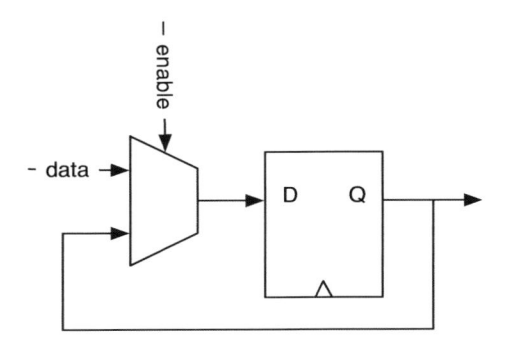

Figure 6.4: A D flip-flop based register with an enable signal.

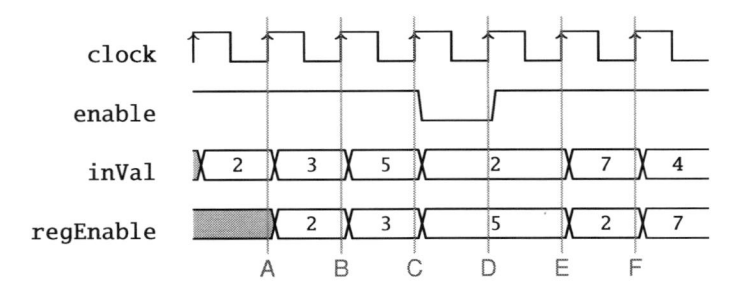

Figure 6.5: A waveform diagram for a register with an enable signal.

pecially in more complex circuits where many operations happen in parallel and data move pipelined through the circuit, timing diagrams are convenient. Chisel testers can also produce waveforms during testing that can be displayed with a waveform viewer and used for debugging.

A typical design pattern is a register with an enable signal. Only when the enable signal is true (high), the register captures the input; otherwise, it keeps its old value. The enable can be implemented, similar to the synchronous reset, with a multiplexer at the input of the register. One input to the multiplexer is the feedback of the output of the register.

Figure 6.4 shows the schematics of a register with enable. As this is also a common design pattern, modern FPGA flip-flops contain a dedicated enable input, and no additional resources are needed.

Figure 6.5 shows an example waveform for a register with enable. Most of the time,

46

6.2 Counters

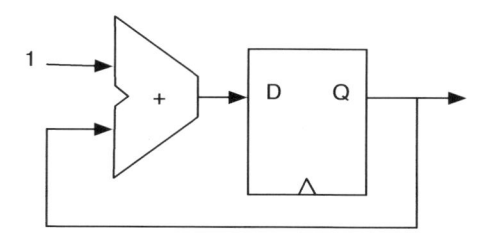

Figure 6.6: An adder and a register result in counter.

enable it high (true) and the register follows the input with one clock cycle delay. Only in the fourth clock cycle enable is low, and the register keeps its value (5) at rising edge D.

A register with an enable can be described in a few lines of Chisel code with a conditional update:

```
val enableReg = Reg(UInt(4.W))

when (enable) {
  enableReg := inVal
}
```

A register with enable can also be reset:

```
val resetEnableReg = RegInit(0.U(4.W))

when (enable) {
  resetEnableReg := inVal
}
```

A register can also be part of an expression. Following circuit detects the rising edge of a signal by comparing its current value with the one from the last clock cycle.

```
val risingEdge = din & !RegNext(din)
```

Now that we have explored all basic uses of a register, we put those registers to good use and build more interesting sequential circuits.

6.2 Counters

One of the most basic sequential circuits is a counter. In its simplest form, a counter is a register where the output is connected to an adder and the adder's output is connected to the input of the register. Figure 6.6 shows such a free-running counter.

A free-running counter with a 4-bit register counts from 0 to 15 and then wraps around to 0 again. A counter shall also be reset to a known value.

```
val cntReg = RegInit(0.U(4.W))

cntReg := cntReg + 1.U
```

When we want to count events, we use a condition to increment the counter.

```
val cntEventsReg = RegInit(0.U(4.W))
when(event) {
  cntEventsReg := cntEventsReg + 1.U
}
```

6.2.1 Counting Up and Down

To count up to a value and then restart with 0, we need to compare the counter value with a maximum constant, e.g., with a when conditional statement.

```
val cntReg = RegInit(0.U(8.W))

cntReg := cntReg + 1.U
when(cntReg === N) {
  cntReg := 0.U
}
```

We can also use a multiplexer for our counter:

```
val cntReg = RegInit(0.U(8.W))

cntReg := Mux(cntReg === N, 0.U, cntReg + 1.U)
```

If we are in the mood of counting down, we start (reset the counter register) with the maximum value and reset the counter to that value when reaching 0.

```
val cntReg = RegInit(N)
```

6.2 Counters

```
cntReg := cntReg - 1.U
when(cntReg === 0.U) {
  cntReg := N
}
```

As we are writing and using more counters, we can define a function with a parameter to generate a counter for us.

```
// This function returns a counter
def genCounter(n: Int) = {
  val cntReg = RegInit(0.U(8.W))
  cntReg := Mux(cntReg === n.U, 0.U, cntReg + 1.U)
  cntReg
}

// now we can easily create many counters
val count10 = genCounter(10)
val count99 = genCounter(99)
```

The last statement of the function genCounter is the return value of the function, in this example, the counting register cntReg.

Note, that in all the examples our counter had values between 0 and N, including N. If we want to count 10 clock cycles we need to set N to 9. Setting N to 10 would be a classic example of an off-by-one error[6].

6.2.2 Generating Timing with Counters

Besides counting events, counters are often used to generate timing. A synchronous circuit runs with a clock with a fixed frequency. The circuit proceeds in those clock ticks. There is no notion of time in a digital circuit other than counting clock ticks. If we know the clock frequency, we can generate circuits that generate timed events, such as blinking a LED at some frequency as we have shown in the Chisel "Hello World" example.

A common practice is to generate single-cycle *ticks* with a frequency f_{tick} that we need in our circuit. That tick occurs every *n* clock cycles, where $n = f_{clock}/f_{tick}$ and the tick is precisely one clock cycle long. This tick is *not* used as a derived clock, but as an enable signal for registers in the circuit that shall logically operate at frequency f_{tick}. Figure 6.7 shows an example of a tick generated every 3 clock cycles.

---

[6]https://en.wikipedia.org/wiki/Off-by-one_error

6 SEQUENTIAL BUILDING BLOCKS

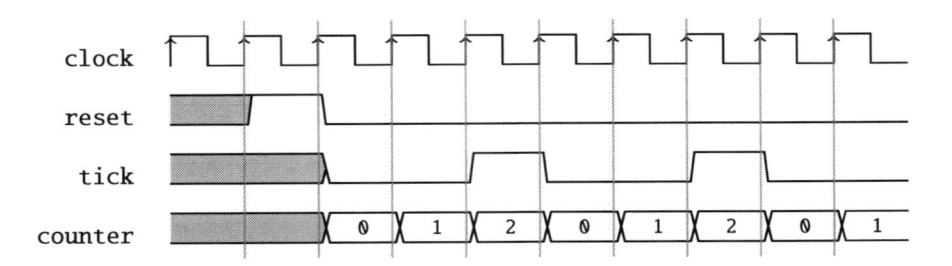

Figure 6.7: A waveform diagram for the generation of a slow frequency tick.

In the following circuit, we describe a counter that counts from 0 to the maximum value of N - 1. When the maximum value is reached, the tick is true for a single cycle, and the counter is reset to 0. When we count from 0 to N - 1, we generate one logical tick every N clock cycles.

```
val tickCounterReg = RegInit(0.U(4.W))
val tick = tickCounterReg === (N-1).U

tickCounterReg := tickCounterReg + 1.U
when (tick) {
  tickCounterReg := 0.U
}
```

This logical timing of one tick every *n* clock cycles can then be used to advance other parts of our circuit with this slower, logical clock. In the following code, we use just another counter that increments by 1 every *n* clock cycles.

```
val lowFrequCntReg = RegInit(0.U(4.W))
when (tick) {
  lowFrequCntReg := lowFrequCntReg + 1.U
}
```

Examples of the usage of this slower *logical* clock are: blinking an LED, generating the baud rate for a serial bus, generating signals for 7-segment display multiplexing, and subsampling input values for debouncing of buttons and switches.

Although width inference should size the registers, it is better to explicitly specify the width with the type at register definition or with the initialization value. Explicit width definition can avoid surprises when a reset value of 0.U results in a counter with a width of a single bit.

6.2.3 The Nerd Counter

Many of us feel like being a nerd[7], sometimes. For example, we want to design a highly optimized version of our counter/tick generation. A standard counter needs following resources: one register, one adder (or subtractor), and a comparator. We cannot do much about the register or the adder. If we count up, we need to compare against a number, which is a bit string. The comparator can be built out of inverters for the zeros in the bit string and a large AND gate. When counting down to zero, the comparator is a large NOR gate, which might be a little bit cheaper than the comparator against a constant in an ASIC. In an FPGA, where logic is built out of lookup tables, there is no difference between comparing against a 0 or 1 bit. The resource requirement is the same for the up and down counter.

However, there is still one more trick a clever hardware designer can pull off. Counting up or down needed a comparison against all counting bits, so far. What if we count from N-2 down to -1? A negative number has the most significant bit set to 1, and a positive number has this bit set to 0. We need to check this bit only to detect that our counter reached -1. Here it is, the counter created by a nerd:

```
val MAX = (N - 2).S(8.W)
val cntReg = RegInit(MAX)
io.tick := false.B

cntReg := cntReg - 1.S
when(cntReg(7)) {
  cntReg := MAX
  io.tick := true.B
}
```

6.3 Memory

A memory can be built out of a collection of registers, in Chisel a Reg of a Vec. However, this is expensive in hardware, and larger memory structures are built as SRAM[8]. For an ASIC, a memory compiler constructs memories. FPGAs contain on-chip memory blocks, also called block RAMs. Those on-chip memory blocks can be combined for larger memories. Memories in an FPGA usually have one read and one write port, or two ports where the direction can be switched.

---

[7]https://en.wikipedia.org/wiki/Nerd
[8]https://en.wikipedia.org/wiki/Static_random-access_memory

6 SEQUENTIAL BUILDING BLOCKS

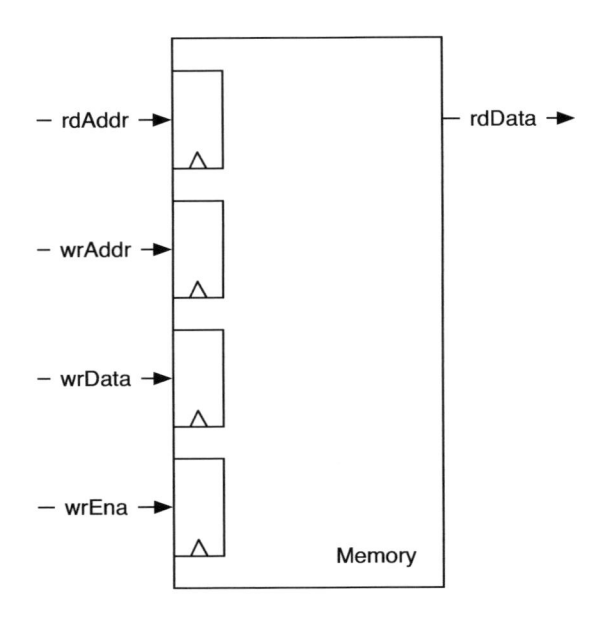

Figure 6.8: A synchronous memory.

FPGAs (and also ASICs) usually support synchronous memories. Synchronous memories have registers on their inputs (read and write address, write data, and write enable). That means the read data is available one clock cycle after setting the address.

Figure 6.8 shows the schematics of such a synchronous memory. The memory is dual-ported with one read port and one write port. The read port has a single input, the read address (`rdAddr`) and one output, the read data (`rdData`). The write port has three inputs: the address (`wrAddr`), the data to be written (`wrData`), and a write enable (`wrEna`). Note that for all inputs, there is a register within the memory showing the synchronous behavior.

To support on-chip memory, Chisel provides the memory constructor `SyncReadMem`. Listing 6.1 shows a component `Memory` that implements 1 KB of memory with byte-wide input and output data and a write enable.

An interesting question is which value is returned from a read when in the same clock cycle a new value is written the same address that is read out. We are interested in the read-during-write behavior of the memory. There are three possibilities: the newly written value, the old value, or undefined (which might be a mix of some bits from the old value and some of the newly written data). Which possibility is available in an

6.3 MEMORY

```
class Memory() extends Module {
  val io = IO(new Bundle {
    val rdAddr = Input(UInt(10.W))
    val rdData = Output(UInt(8.W))
    val wrEna = Input(Bool())
    val wrData = Input(UInt(8.W))
    val wrAddr = Input(UInt(10.W))
  })

  val mem = SyncReadMem(1024, UInt(8.W))

  io.rdData := mem.read(io.rdAddr)

  when(io.wrEna) {
    mem.write(io.wrAddr, io.wrData)
  }
}
```

Listing 6.1: 1 KB of synchronous memory.

FPGA depends on the FPGA type and sometimes can be specified. Chisel documents that the read data is undefined.

If we want to read out the newly written value, we can build a forwarding circuit that detects that the addresses are equal and *forwards* the write data. Figure 6.9 shows the memory with the forwarding circuit. Read and write addresses are compared and gated with the write enable to select between the forwarding path of the write data or the memory read data. The write data is delayed by one clock cycle with a register.

Listing 6.2 shows the Chisel code for a synchronous memory including the forwarding circuit. We need to store the write data into a register (wrDataReg) to be available in the next clock cycle the synchronous memory also has a one clock cycle latency. We compare the two input addresses (wrAddr and rdAddr) and check if wrEna is true for the forwarding condition. That condition is also delayed by one clock cycle. A multiplexer selects between the forwarding (write) data or the read data from memory.

Chisel also provides Mem, which represents a memory with synchronous write and an asynchronous read. As this memory type is usually not directly available in an FPGA, the synthesize tool will build it out of flip-flops. Therefore, we recommend using SyncReadMem.

53

6 Sequential Building Blocks

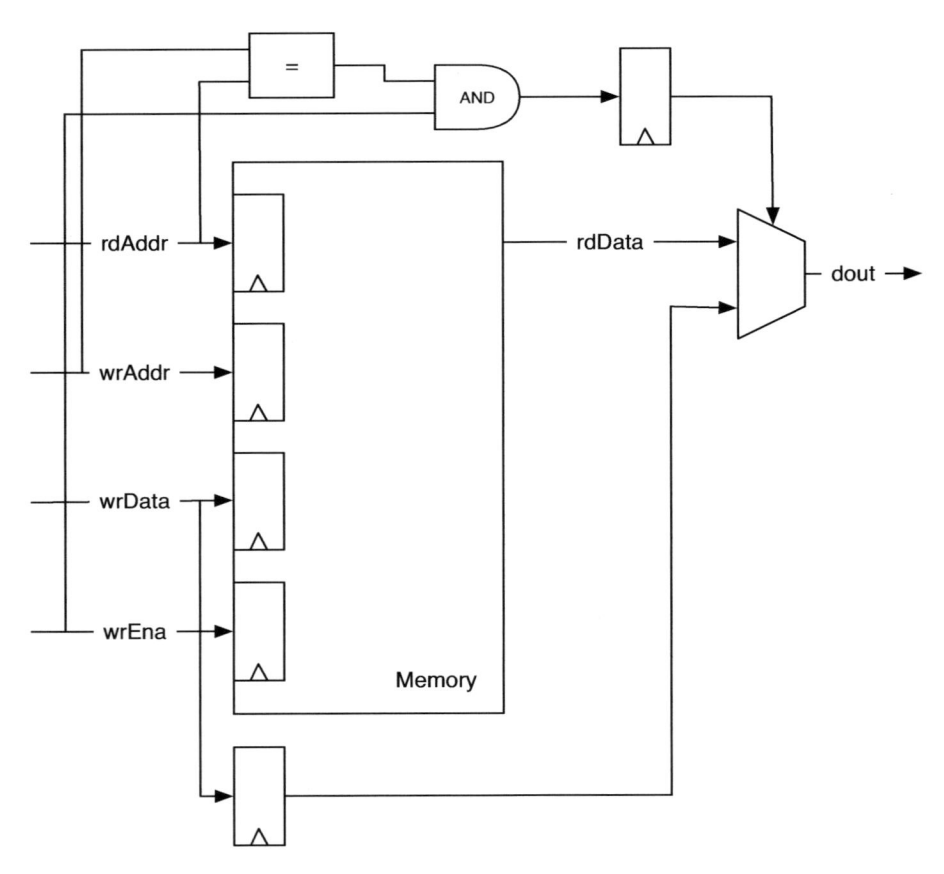

Figure 6.9: A synchronous memory with forwarding for a defined read-during-write behavior.

```
class ForwardingMemory() extends Module {
  val io = IO(new Bundle {
    val rdAddr = Input(UInt(10.W))
    val rdData = Output(UInt(8.W))
    val wrEna = Input(Bool())
    val wrData = Input(UInt(8.W))
    val wrAddr = Input(UInt(10.W))
  })

  val mem = SyncReadMem(1024, UInt(8.W))

  val wrDataReg = RegNext(io.wrData)
  val doForwardReg = RegNext(io.wrAddr === io.rdAddr &&
      io.wrEna)

  val memData = mem.read(io.rdAddr)

  when(io.wrEna) {
    mem.write(io.wrAddr, io.wrData)
  }

  io.rdData := Mux(doForwardReg, wrDataReg, memData)
}
```

Listing 6.2: A memory with a forwarding circuit.

6.4 Exercise

Use the 7-segment encoder from the last exercise and add a 4-bit counter as input to switch the display from 0 to F. When you directly connect this counter to the clock of the FPGA board, you will see all 16 numbers overlapped (all 7 segments will light up). Therefore, you need to slow down the counting. Create a second counter that can generate a single-cycle *tick* signal every 500 milliseconds. Use that signal as enable signal for the 4-bit counter.

7 Finite-State Machines

A finite-state machine (FSM) is a basic building block in digital design. An FSM can be described as a set of *states* and conditional (guarded) *state transitions* between states. An FSM has an initial state, which is set on reset. FSMs are also called synchronous sequential circuits.

An implementation of an FSM consists of three parts: (1) a register that holds the current state, (2) combinational logic that computes the next state that depends on the current state and the input, and (3) combinational logic that computes the output of the FSM.

In principle, every digital circuit that contains a register or other memory elements to store state can be described as a single FSM. However, this might not be practical, e.g., try to describe your laptop as a single FSM. In the next chapter, we describe how to build larger systems out of smaller FSMs by combining them into communicating FSMs.

7.1 Basic Finite-State Machine

Figure 7.1 shows the schematics of an FSM. The register contains the current state. The next state logic computes the next state value (next_state) from the current state and the input (in). On the next clock tick, state becomes next_state. The output logic

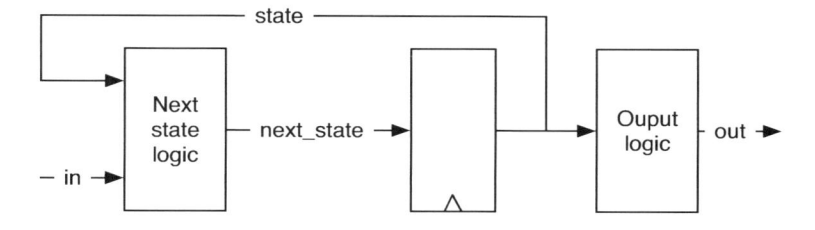

Figure 7.1: A finite state machine (Moore type).

7 Finite-State Machines

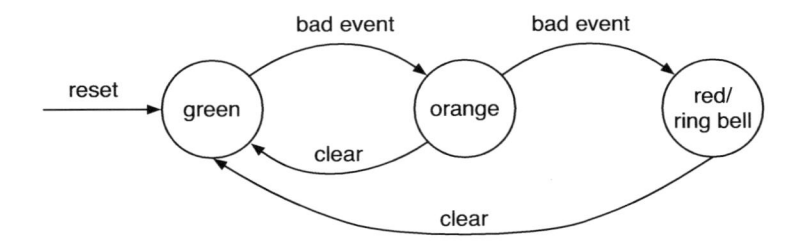

Figure 7.2: The state diagram of an alarm FSM.

computes the output (out). As the output depends on the current state only, this state machine is called a Moore machine[1].

A state diagram[2] describes the behavior of such an FSM visually. In a state diagram, individual states are depicted as circles labeled with the state names. State transitions are shown with arrows between states. The guard (or condition) when this transition is taken is drawn as a label for the arrow.

Figure 7.2 shows the state diagram of a simple example FSM. The FSM has three states: *green*, *orange*, and *red*, indicating a level of alarm. The FSM starts at the *green* level. When a *bad event* happens the alarm level is switched to *orange*. On a second bad event, the alarm level is switched to *red*. In that case, we want to ring a bell; *ring bell* it the only output of this FSM. We add the output to the *red* state. The alarm can be reset with a *clear* signal.

Although a state diagram may be visually pleasing and the function of an FSM can be grasped quickly, a state table may be quicker to write down. Table 7.1 shows the state table for our alarm FSM. We list the current state, the input values, the resulting next state, and the output value for the current state. In principle, we would need to specify all possible inputs for all possible states. This table would have $3 \times 4 = 12$ rows. We simplify the table by indicating that the *clear* input is a don't care when a *bad event* happens. That means *bad event* has priority over *clear*. The output column has some repetition. If we have a larger FSM and/or more outputs, we can split the table into two, one for the next state logic and one for the output logic.

Finally, after all the design of our warning level FSM, we shall code it in Chisel. Listing 7.1 shows the Chisel code for the alarm FSM. Note, that we use the Chisel type Bool for the inputs and the output of the FSM. To use Enum and the switch control instruction, we need to import chisel3.util._.

---

[1] https://en.wikipedia.org/wiki/Moore_machine
[2] https://en.wikipedia.org/wiki/State_diagram

7.1 Basic Finite-State Machine

```
import chisel3._
import chisel3.util._

class SimpleFsm extends Module {
  val io = IO(new Bundle{
    val badEvent = Input(Bool())
    val clear = Input(Bool())
    val ringBell = Output(Bool())
  })

  // The three states
  val green :: orange :: red :: Nil = Enum(3)

  // The state register
  val stateReg = RegInit(green)

  // Next state logic
  switch (stateReg) {
    is (green) {
      when(io.badEvent) {
        stateReg := orange
      }
    }
    is (orange) {
      when(io.badEvent) {
        stateReg := red
      } .elsewhen(io.clear) {
        stateReg := green
      }
    }
    is (red) {
      when (io.clear) {
        stateReg := green
      }
    }
  }

  // Output logic
  io.ringBell := stateReg === red
}
```

Listing 7.1: The Chisel code for the alarm FSM.

7 FINITE-STATE MACHINES

Table 7.1: State table for the alarm FSM.

State	Bad event	Clear	Next state	Ring bell
green	0	0	green	0
green	1	-	orange	0
orange	0	0	orange	0
orange	1	-	red	0
orange	0	1	green	0
red	0	0	red	1
red	0	1	green	1

The complete Chisel code for this simple FSM fits into one page. Let us step through the individual parts. The FSM has two input and a single output signal, captured in a Chisel `Bundle`:

```
val io = IO(new Bundle{
  val badEvent = Input(Bool())
  val clear = Input(Bool())
  val ringBell = Output(Bool())
})
```

Quite some work has been spent in optimal state encoding. Two common options are binary or one-hot encoding. However, we leave those low-level decisions to the synthesize tool and aim for readable code.[3] Therefore, we use an enumeration type with symbolic names for the states:

```
val green :: orange :: red :: Nil = Enum(3)
```

The individual state values are described as a list where the individual elements are concatenated with the :: operator; `Nil` represents the end of the list. An `Enum` instance is *assigned* to the list of states. The register holding the state is defined with the *green* state as the reset value:

```
val stateReg = RegInit(green)
```

The meat of the FSM is in the next state logic. We use a Chisel switch on the state

---

[3] In the current version of Chisel the `Enum` type represents states in binary encoding. If we want a different encoding, e.g., one-hot encoding, we can define Chisel constants for the state names.

register to cover all states. Within each is branch we code the next state logic, which depends on the inputs, by assigning a new value for our state register:

```
switch (stateReg) {
  is (green) {
    when(io.badEvent) {
      stateReg := orange
    }
  }
  is (orange) {
    when(io.badEvent) {
      stateReg := red
    } .elsewhen(io.clear) {
      stateReg := green
    }
  }
  is (red) {
    when (io.clear) {
      stateReg := green
    }
  }
}
```

Last, but not least, we code our *ringing bell* output to be true when the state is *red*.

```
io.ringBell := stateReg === red
```

Note that we did *not* introduce a next_state signal for the register input, as it is common practice in Verilog or VHDL. Registers in Verilog and VHDL are described in a special syntax and cannot be assigned (and reassigned) within a combinational block. Therefore, the additional signal, computed in a combinational block, is introduced and connected to the register input. In Chisel a register is a base type and can be freely used within a combinational block.

7.2 Faster Output with a Mealy FSM

On a Moore FSM, the output depends only on the current state. That means that a change of an input can be seen as a change of the output *earliest* in the next clock cycle. If we want to observe an immediate change, we need a combinational path from the input to the output. Let us consider a minimal example, an edge detection circuit. We have seen this Chisel one-liner before:

7 Finite-State Machines

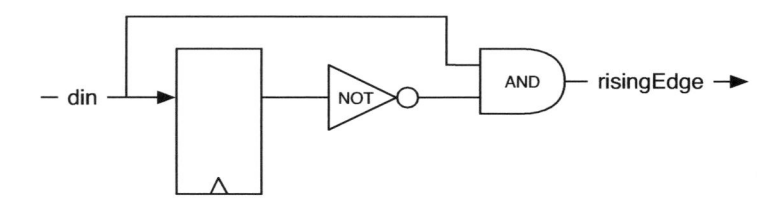

Figure 7.3: A rising edge detector (Mealy type FSM).

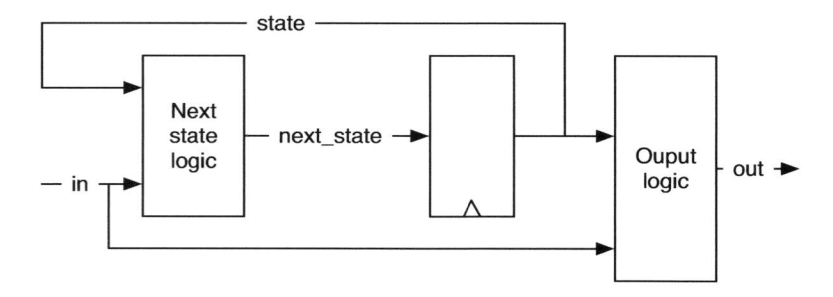

Figure 7.4: A Mealy type finite state machine.

```
val risingEdge = din & !RegNext(din)
```

Figure 7.7 shows the schematic of the rising edge detector. The output becomes 1 for one clock cycle when the current input is 1 and the input in the last clock cycle was 0. The state register is just a single D flip-flop where the next state is just the input. We can also consider this as a delay element of one clock cycle. The output logic *compares* the current input with the current state.

When the output depends also on the input, i.e., there is a combinational path between the input of the FSM and the output, this is called a Mealy machine[4].

Figure 7.4 shows the schematic of a Mealy type FSM. Similar to the Moore FSM, the register contains the current state, and the next state logic computes the next state value (next_state) from the current state and the input (in). On the next clock tick, state becomes next_state. The output logic computes the output (out) from the current state *and* the input to the FSM.

Figure 7.5 shows the state diagram of the Mealy FSM for the edge detector. As the

---
[4]https://en.wikipedia.org/wiki/Mealy_machine

7.2 FASTER OUTPUT WITH A MEALY FSM

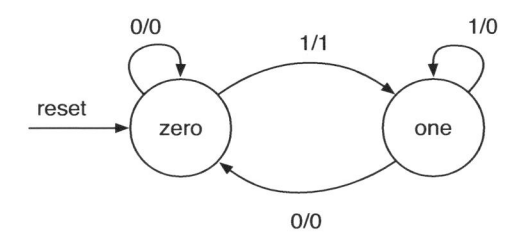

Figure 7.5: The state diagram of the rising edge detector as Mealy FSM.

state register consists just of a single D flip-flop, only two states are possible, which we name zero and one in this example. As the output of a Mealy FSM does not only depend on the state, but also on the input, we cannot describe the output as part of the state circle. Instead, the transitions between the states are labeled with the input value (condition) *and* the output (after the slash). Note also that we draw self transitions, e.g., in state zero when the input is 0 the FSM stays in state zero, and the output is 0. The rising edge FSM generates the 1 output only on the transition from state zero to state one. In state one, which represents that the input is now 1, the output is 0. We only want a single (cycle) puls for each rising edge of the input.

Listing 7.2 shows the Chisel code for the rising edge detection with a Mealy machine. As in the previous example, we use the Chisel type Bool for the single-bit input and output. The output logic is now part of the next state logic; on the transition from zero to one, the output is set to true.B. Otherwise, the default assignment to the output (false.B) counts.

One can ask if a full-blown FSM is the best solution for the edge detection circuit, especially, as we have seen a Chisel one-liner for the same functionality. The hardware consumptions is similar. Both solutions need a single D flip-flop for the state. The combinational logic for the FSM is probably a bit more complicated, as the state change depends on the current state and the input value. For this function, the one-liner is easier to write and easier to read, which is more important. Therefore, the one-liner is the preferred solution.

We have used this example to show one of the smallest possible Mealy FSMs. FSMs shall be used for more complex circuits with three and more states.

```scala
import chisel3._
import chisel3.util._

class RisingFsm extends Module {
  val io = IO(new Bundle{
    val din = Input(Bool())
    val risingEdge = Output(Bool())
  })

  // The two states
  val zero :: one :: Nil = Enum(2)

  // The state register
  val stateReg = RegInit(zero)

  // default value for output
  io.risingEdge := false.B

  // Next state and output logic
  switch (stateReg) {
    is(zero) {
      when(io.din) {
        stateReg := one
        io.risingEdge := true.B
      }
    }
    is(one) {
      when(!io.din) {
        stateReg := zero
      }
    }
  }
}
```

Listing 7.2: Rising edge detection with a Mealy FSM.

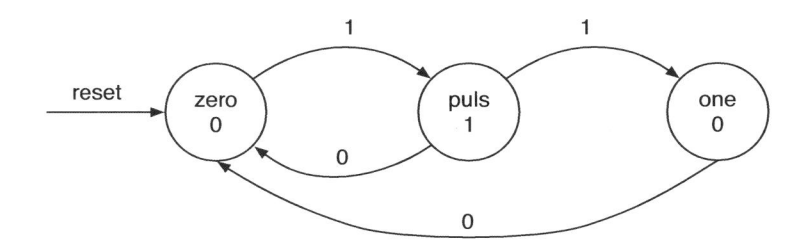

Figure 7.6: The state diagram of the rising edge detector as Moore FSM.

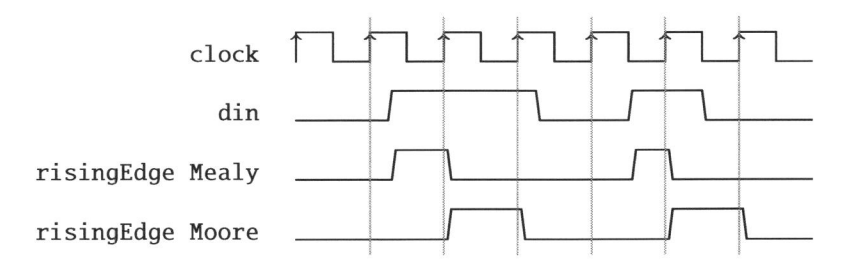

Figure 7.7: Mealy and a Moore FSM waveform for rising edge detection.

7.3 Moore versus Mealy

To show the difference between a Moore and Mealy FSM, we redo the edge detection with a Moore FSM.

Figure 7.6 shows the state diagram for the rising edge detection with a Moore FSM. The first thing to notice is that the Moore FSM needs three states, compared to two states in the Mealy version. The state puls is needed to produce the single-cycle puls. The FSM stays in state puls just one clock cycle and then proceeds either back to the start state zero or to the one state, waiting for the input to become 0 again. We show the input condition on the state transition arrows and the FSM output within the state representing circles.

Listing 7.3 shows the Moore version of the rising edge detection circuit. Is uses double the number of D flip-flops than the Mealy or direct coded version. The resulting next state logic is therefore also larger than the Mealy or direct coded version.

Figure 7.7 shows the waveform of a Mealy and a Moore version of the rising edge detection FSM. We can see that the Mealy output closely follows the input rising edge, while the Moore output rises after the clock tick. We can also see that the Moore output

7 Finite-State Machines

```
import chisel3._
import chisel3.util._

class RisingMooreFsm extends Module {
  val io = IO(new Bundle{
    val din = Input(Bool())
    val risingEdge = Output(Bool())
  })

  // The three states
  val zero :: puls :: one :: Nil = Enum(3)

  // The state register
  val stateReg = RegInit(zero)

  // Next state logic
  switch (stateReg) {
    is(zero) {
      when(io.din) {
        stateReg := puls
      }
    }
    is(puls) {
      when(io.din) {
        stateReg := one
      } .otherwise {
        stateReg := zero
      }
    }
    is(one) {
      when(!io.din) {
        stateReg := zero
      }
    }
  }

  // Output logic
  io.risingEdge := stateReg === puls
}
```

Listing 7.3: Rising edge detection with a Moore FSM.

is one clock cycle wide, where the Mealy output is usually less than a clock cycle.

From the above example, one is tempted to find Mealy FSMs the *better* FSMs as they need less state (and therefore logic) and react faster than a Moore FSM. However, the combinational path within a Mealy machine can cause trouble in larger designs. First, with a chain of communicating FSM (see next chapter), this combinational path can become lengthy. Second, if the communicating FSMs build a circle, the result is a combinational loop, which is an error in synchronous design. Due to a cut in the combinational path with the state register in a Moore FSM, all the above issues do not exist for communicating Moore FSMs.

In summary, Moore FSMs combine better for communicating state machines; they are *more robust* than Mealy FSMs. Use Mealy FSMs only when the reaction within the same cycle is of utmost importance. Small circuits such as the rising edge detection, which are practically Mealy machines, are fine as well.

7.4 Exercise

In this chapter, you have seen many examples of very small FSMs. Now it is time to write some *real* FSM code. Pick a little bit more complex example and implement the FSM and write a test bench for it.

A classic example for a FSM is a traffic light controller (see [3, Section 14.3]). A traffic light controller has to ensure that on a switch from red to green there is a phase in between where both roads in the intersection have a no-go light (red and orange). To make this example a little bit more interesting, consider a priority road. The minor road has two car detectors (on both entries into the intersection). Switch to green for the minor road only when a car is detected and then switch back to green for the priority road.

8 Communicating State Machines

A problem is often too complex to describe it with a single FSM. In that case, the problem can be divided into two or more smaller and simpler FSMs. Those FSMs then communicate with signals. One FSMs output is another FSMs input, and the FSM watches the output of the other FSM. When we split a large FSM into simpler ones, this is called factoring FSMs. However, often communicating FSMs are directly designed from the specification, as often a single FSM would be infeasible large.

8.1 A Light Flasher Example

To discuss communicating FSMs, we use an example from [3, Chapter 17], the light flasher. The light flasher has one input start and one output light. The specification of the light flasher is as follows:

- when start is high for one clock cycle, the flashing sequence starts;
- the sequence is to flash three times;
- where the light goes *on* for six clock cycles, and the light goes *off* for four clock cycles between flashes;
- after the sequence, the FSM switches the light *off* and waits for the next start.

The FSM for a direct implementation[1] has 27 states: one initial state that is waiting for the input, 3×6 states for the three *on* states and 2×4 states for the *off* states. We do not show the code for this simple-minded implementation of the light flasher.

The problem can be solved more elegantly by factoring this large FSM into two smaller FSMs: the master FSM implements the flashing logic, and the timer FSM implements the waiting. Figure 8.1 shows the composition of the two FSMs.

The timer FSM counts down for 6 or 4 clock cycles to produce the desired timing. The timer specification is as follows:

---
[1]The state diagram is shown in [3, p. 376].

8 COMMUNICATING STATE MACHINES

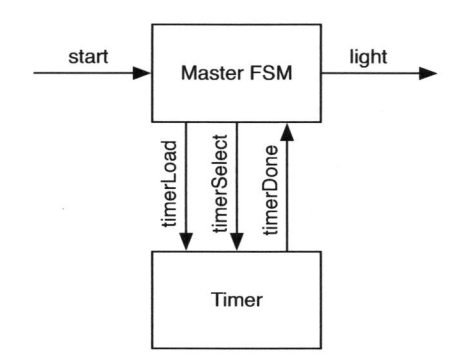

Figure 8.1: The light flasher split into a Master FSM and a Timer FSM.

- when `timerLoad` is asserted, the timer loads a value into the down counter, independent of the state;

- `timerSelect` selects between 5 or 3 for the load;

- `timerDone` is asserted when the counter completed the countdown and remains asserted;

- otherwise, the timer counts down.

Following code shows the timer FSM of the light flasher:

```
val timerReg = RegInit(0.U)
timerDone := timerReg === 0.U

// Timer FSM (down counter)
when(!timerDone) {
  timerReg := timerReg - 1.U
}
when (timerLoad) {
  when (timerSelect) {
    timerReg := 5.U
  } .otherwise {
    timerReg := 3.U
  }
}
```

```
val off :: flash1 :: space1 :: flash2 :: space2 :: flash3 ::
    Nil = Enum(6)
val stateReg = RegInit(off)

val light = WireInit(false.B) // FSM output

// Timer connection
val timerLoad = WireInit(false.B) // start timer with a load
val timerSelect = WireInit(true.B) // select 6 or 4 cycles
val timerDone = Wire(Bool())

timerLoad := timerDone

// Master FSM
switch(stateReg) {
  is(off) {
    timerLoad := true.B
    timerSelect := true.B
    when (start) { stateReg := flash1 }
  }
  is (flash1) {
    timerSelect := false.B
    light := true.B
    when (timerDone) { stateReg := space1 }
  }
  is (space1) {
    when (timerDone) { stateReg := flash2 }
  }
  is (flash2) {
    timerSelect := false.B
    light := true.B
    when (timerDone) { stateReg := space2 }
  }
  is (space2) {
    when (timerDone) { stateReg := flash3 }
  }
  is (flash3) {
    timerSelect := false.B
    light := true.B
    when (timerDone) { stateReg := off }
  }
}
```

Listing 8.1: Master FSM of the light flasher.

8 Communicating State Machines

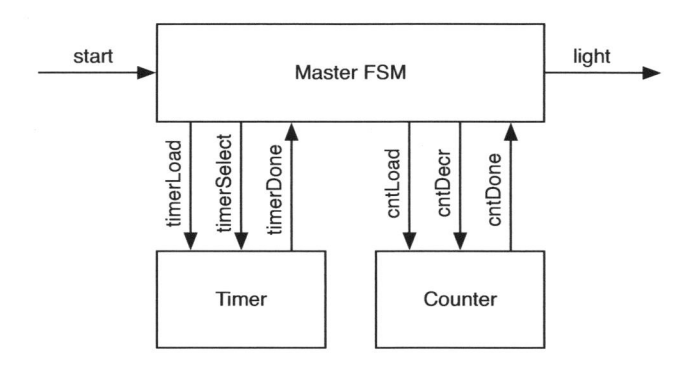

Figure 8.2: The light flasher split into a Master FSM, a Timer FSM, and a Counter FSM.

Listing 8.1 shows the master FSM.

This solution with a master FSM and a timer has still redundancy in the code of the master FSM. States `flash1`, `flash2`, and `flash3` are performing the same function, states `space1` and `space2` as well. We can factor out the number of remaining flashes into a second counter. Then the master FSM is reduced to three states: `off`, `flash`, and `space`.

Figure 8.2 shows the design with a master FSM and two FSMs that count: one FSM to count clock cycles for the interval length of *on* and *off*; the second FSM to count the remaining flashes.

Following code shows the down counter FSM:

```
val cntReg = RegInit(0.U)
cntDone := cntReg === 0.U

// Down counter FSM
when(cntLoad) { cntReg := 2.U }
when(cntDecr) { cntReg := cntReg - 1.U }
```

Note, that the counter is loaded with 2 for 3 flashes, as it counts the *remaining* flashes and is decremented in state `space` when the timer is done. Listing 8.2 shows the master FSM for the double refactored flasher.

Besides having a master FSM that is reduced to just three states, our current solution is also better configurable. No FSM needs to be changed if we want to change the length of the *on* or *off* intervals or the number of flashes.

In this section, we have explored communicating circuits, especially FSM, that only

8.1 A Light Flasher Example

```
val off :: flash :: space :: Nil = Enum(3)
val stateReg = RegInit(off)

val light = WireInit(false.B) // FSM output

// Timer connection
val timerLoad = WireInit(false.B) // start timer with a load
val timerSelect = WireInit(true.B) // select 6 or 4 cycles
val timerDone = Wire(Bool())
// Counter connection
val cntLoad = WireInit(false.B)
val cntDecr = WireInit(false.B)
val cntDone = Wire(Bool())

timerLoad := timerDone

switch(stateReg) {
  is(off) {
    timerLoad := true.B
    timerSelect := true.B
    cntLoad := true.B
    when (start) { stateReg := flash }
  }
  is (flash) {
    timerSelect := false.B
    light := true.B
    when (timerDone & !cntDone) { stateReg := space }
    when (timerDone & cntDone) { stateReg := off }
  }
  is (space) {
    cntDecr := timerDone
    when (timerDone) { stateReg := flash }
  }
}
```

Listing 8.2: Master FSM of the double refactored light flasher.

8 Communicating State Machines

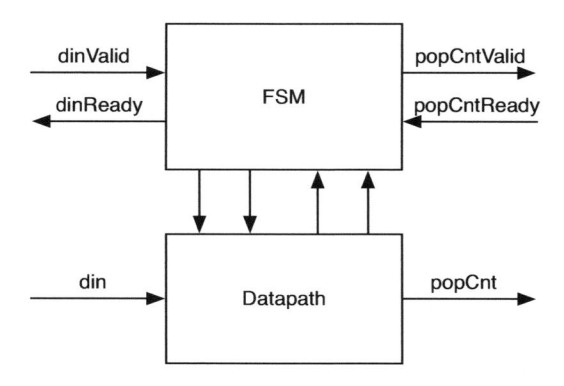

Figure 8.3: A state machine with a datapath.

exchange control signals. However, circuits can also exchange data. For the coordinated exchange of data, we use handshake signals. The next section describes the ready-valid interface for flow control of unidirectional data exchange.

8.2 State Machine with Datapath

One typical example of communicating state machines is a state machine combined with a datapath. This combination is often called a finite state machine with datapath (FSMD). The state machine controls the datapath, and the datapath performs the computation. The FSM input is the input from the environment and the input from the datapath. The data from the environment is fed into the datapath, and the data output comes from the datapath. Figure 8.3 shows an example of the combination of the FSM with the datapath.

8.2.1 Popcount Example

The FSMD shown in Figure 8.3 serves as an example that computes the popcount, also called the Hamming weight[2]. The Hamming weight is the number of symbols different from the zero symbol. For a binary string, this is the number of '1's.

The popcount unit contains the data input din and the result output popCount, both connected to the datapath. For the input and the output we use a ready-valid handshake.

---

[2]https://en.wikipedia.org/wiki/Hamming_weight

8.2 STATE MACHINE WITH DATAPATH

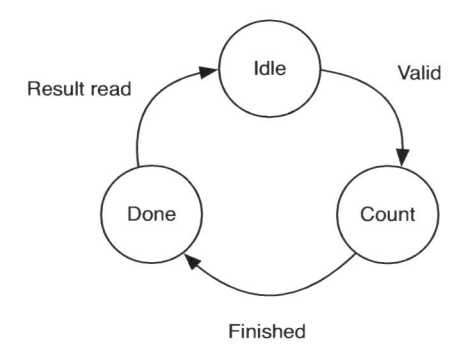

Figure 8.4: State diagram for the popcount FSM.

When data is available, valid is asserted. When a receiver can accept data it asserts ready. When both signals are asserted the transfer takes place. The handshake signals are connected to the FSM. The FSM is connected with the datapath with control signals towards the datapath and with status signals from the datapath.

As a next step, we can design the FSM, starting with a state diagram, shown in Figure 8.4. We start in state Idle, where the FSM waits for input. When data arrives, signaled with a valid signal, the FSM advances to state Load to load a shift register. The FSM proceeds to the next state Count, there the number of '1's is counted sequentially. We use a shift register, an adder, an accumulator register, and a down counter to perform the computation. When the down counter reaches zero, we are finished and the FSM moves to state Done. There the FSM signals with a valid signal that the popcount value is ready to be consumed. On a ready signal from the receiver, the FSM moves back to the Idle state, ready to compute the next popcount.

The top level component, shown in Listing 8.3 instantiates the FSM and the datapath components and connects them with bulk connections.

Figure 8.5 shows the datapath for the popcount circuit. The data is loaded into the shf register. On the load also the cnt register is reset to 0. To count the number of '1's, the shf register is shifted right, and the least significant bit is added to cnt each clock cycle. A counter, not shown in the figure, counts down until all bits have been shifted through the least significant bit. When the counter reaches zero, the popcount has finished. The FSM switches to state Done and signals the result by asserting popCntReady. When the result is read, signaled by asserting popCntValid the FSW switches back to Idle.

On a load signal, the regData register is loaded with the input, the regPopCount register reset to 0, and the counter register regCount set to the number of shifts to be

8 Communicating State Machines

```
class PopCount extends Module {
  val io = IO(new Bundle {
    val dinValid = Input(Bool())
    val dinReady = Output(Bool())
    val din = Input(UInt(8.W))
    val popCntValid = Output(Bool())
    val popCntReady = Input(Bool())
    val popCnt = Output(UInt(4.W))
  })

  val fsm = Module(new PopCountFSM)
  val data = Module(new PopCountDataPath)

  fsm.io.dinValid := io.dinValid
  io.dinReady := fsm.io.dinReady
  io.popCntValid := fsm.io.popCntValid
  fsm.io.popCntReady := io.popCntReady

  data.io.din := io.din
  io.popCnt := data.io.popCnt
  data.io.load := fsm.io.load
  fsm.io.done := data.io.done
}
```

Listing 8.3: The top level of the popcount circuit.

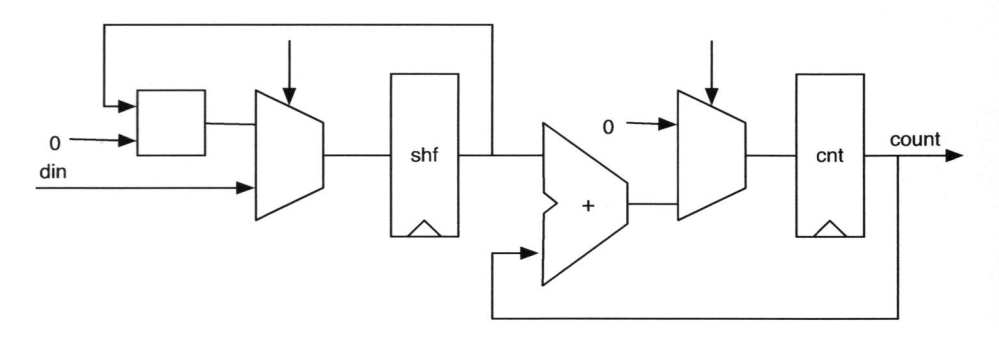

Figure 8.5: Datapath for the popcount circuit.

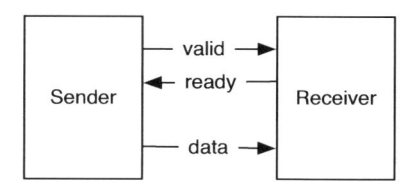

Figure 8.6: The ready-valid flow control.

performed.

Otherwise, the regData register is shifted to the right, the least significant bit of the regData register added to the regPopCount register, and the counter decremented until it is 0. When the counter is 0, the output contains the popcount. Listing 8.4 shows the Chisel code for the datapath of the popcount circuit.

The FSM starts in state idle. On a valid signal for the input data (dinValid) it switches to the count state and waits till the datapath has finished counting. When the popcount is valid, the FSM switches to state done and waits till the popcount is read (signaled by popCntReady). Listing 8.5 shows the code of the FSM.

8.3 Ready-Valid Interface

Communication of subsystems can be generalized to the movement of data and handshaking for flow control. In the popcount example, we have seen a handshaking interface for the input and the output data using valid and ready signals.

The ready-valid interface [3, p. 480] is a simple flow control interface consisting of data and a valid signal at the sender side and a ready signal at the receiver side (see Figure 8.6). The sender asserts valid when data is available, and the receiver asserts ready when it is ready to receive one word of data. The transmission of the data happens when both signals, valid and ready, are asserted. If either of the two signals is not asserted, no transfer takes place.

To make this interface composable neither ready not valid is allowed to depend combinational on the other signal.

```scala
class PopCountDataPath extends Module {
  val io = IO(new Bundle {
    val din = Input(UInt(8.W))
    val load = Input(Bool())
    val popCnt = Output(UInt(4.W))
    val done = Output(Bool())
  })

  val dataReg = RegInit(0.U(8.W))
  val popCntReg = RegInit(0.U(8.W))
  val counterReg= RegInit(0.U(4.W))

  dataReg := 0.U ## dataReg(7, 1)
  popCntReg := popCntReg + dataReg(0)

  val done = counterReg === 0.U
  when (!done) {
    counterReg := counterReg - 1.U
  }

  when(io.load) {
    dataReg := io.din
    popCntReg := 0.U
    counterReg := 8.U
  }

  // debug output
  printf("%x %d\n", dataReg, popCntReg)

  io.popCnt := popCntReg
  io.done := done
}
```

Listing 8.4: Datapath of the popcount circuit.

8.3 READY-VALID INTERFACE

```
class PopCountFSM extends Module {
  val io = IO(new Bundle {
    val dinValid = Input(Bool())
    val dinReady = Output(Bool())
    val popCntValid = Output(Bool())
    val popCntReady = Input(Bool())
    val load = Output(Bool())
    val done = Input(Bool())
  })

  val idle :: count :: done :: Nil = Enum(3)
  val stateReg = RegInit(idle)

  io.load := false.B

  io.dinReady := false.B
  io.popCntValid := false.B

  switch(stateReg) {
    is(idle) {
      io.dinReady := true.B
      when(io.dinValid) {
        io.load := true.B
        stateReg := count
      }
    }
    is(count) {
      when(io.done) {
        stateReg := done
      }
    }
    is(done) {
      io.popCntValid := true.B
      when(io.popCntReady) {
        stateReg := idle
      }
    }
  }
}
```

Listing 8.5: The FSM of the popcount circuit.

9 Hardware Generators

The strength of Chisel is that it allows us to write so-called hardware generators. With older hardware description languages, such as VHDL and Verilog, we usually use another language, e.g., Java or Python, to generate hardware. The author has often written small Java programs to generate VHDL tables. In Chisel, the full power of Scala (and Java libraries) is available at hardware construction. Therefore, we can write our hardware generators in the same language and execute them as part of the Chisel circuit generation.

9.1 Configure with Parameters

Chisel components and functions can be configured with parameters. Parameters can be as simple as an integer constant, but can also be a Chisel hardware type.

9.1.1 Simple Parameters

The basic way to parameterize a circuit is to define a bit width as a parameter. Parameters can be passed as arguments to the constructor of the Chisel module. Following example is a toy example of a module that implements an adder with a configurable bit width. The bit width n is a parameter (of Scala type Int) of the component passed into the constructor that can be used in the IO bundle.

```
class ParamAdder(n: Int) extends Module {
  val io = IO(new Bundle{
    val a = Input(UInt(n.W))
    val b = Input(UInt(n.W))
    val c = Output(UInt(n.W))
  })

  io.c := io.a + io.b
}
```

Parameterized versions of the adder can be created as follows:

```
val add8  = Module(new ParamAdder(8))
val add16 = Module(new ParamAdder(16))
```

9.1.2 Functions with Type Parameters

Having the bit width as a configuration parameter is just the starting point for hardware generators. A very flexible configuration is the usage of types. That feature allows for Chisel to provide a multiplexer (Mux) that can accept any types for the multiplexing. To show how to use types for the configuration, we build a multiplexer that accepts arbitrary types. Following function defines the multiplexer:

```
def myMux[T <: Data](sel: Bool, tPath: T, fPath: T): T = {
  val ret = WireInit(fPath)
  when (sel) {
    ret := tPath
  }
  ret
}
```

Chisel allows parameterizing functions with types, in our case with Chisel types. The expression in the square brackets [T <: Data] defines a type parameter T set is Data or a subclass of Data. Data is the root of the Chisel type system.

Our multiplexer function has three parameters: the boolean condition, one parameter for the true path, and one parameter for the false path. Both path parameters are of type T, an information that is provided at function call. The function itself is straight forward: we define a wire with the default value of fPath and change the value is the condition is true to the tPath. This condition is a classic multiplexer function. At the end of the function, we return the multiplexer hardware.

We can use our multiplexer function with simple types such as UInt:

```
val resA = myMux(selA, 5.U, 10.U)
```

The types of the two multiplexer paths need to be the same. Following wrong usage of the multiplexer results in a runtime error:

```
val resErr = myMux(selA, 5.U, 10.S)
```

We define our type as a Bundle with two fields:

```
class ComplexIO extends Bundle {
```

```
  val d = UInt(10.W)
  val b = Bool()
}
```

We can define `Bundle` constants by first creating a `Wire` and then setting the subfields. Then we can use our parameterized multiplexer with this complex type.

```
val tVal = Wire(new ComplexIO)
tVal.b := true.B
tVal.d := 42.U
val fVal = Wire(new ComplexIO)
fVal.b := false.B
fVal.d := 13.U

// The mulitplexer with a complex type
val resB = myMux(selB, tVal, fVal)
```

In our initial design of the function, we used `WireInit` to create a wire with the type T with a default value. If we need to create a wire just of the Chisel type without using a default value, we can use fPath.cloneType to get the Chisel type. Following function shows the alternative way to code the multiplexer.

```
def myMuxAlt[T <: Data](sel: Bool, tPath: T, fPath: T): T = {
  val ret = Wire(fPath.cloneType)
  ret := fPath
  when (sel) {
    ret := tPath
  }
  ret
}
```

9.1.3 Modules with Type Parameters

We can also parameterize modules with Chisel types. Let us assume we want to design a network-on-chip to move data between different processing cores. However, we do not want to hardcode the data format in the router interface; we want to *parametrize* it. Similar to the type parameter for a function, we add a type parameter T to the Module constructor. Furthermore, we need to have one constructor parameter of that type. Additionally, in this example, we also make the number of router ports configurable.

```
class NocRouter[T <: Data](dt: T, n: Int) extends Module {
  val io =IO(new Bundle {
    val inPort = Input(Vec(n, dt))
    val address = Input(Vec(n, UInt(8.W)))
    val outPort = Output(Vec(n, dt))
  })

  // Route the payload according to the address
  // ...
```

To use our router, we first need to define the data type we want to route, e.g., as a Chisel Bundle:

```
class Payload extends Bundle {
  val data = UInt(16.W)
  val flag = Bool()
}
```

We create a router by passing an instance of the user-defined Bundle and the number of ports to the constructor of the router:

```
val router = Module(new NocRouter(new Payload, 2))
```

9.1.4 Parametrize Bundles

In the router example, we used two different vectors of fields for the input of the router: one for the address and one for the data, which was parameterized. A more elegant solution would be to have a Bundle that itself is parametrized. Something like:

```
class Port[T <: Data](dt: T) extends Bundle {
  val address = UInt(8.W)
  val data = dt.cloneType
}
```

The Bundle has a parameter of type T, which is a subtype of Chisel's Data type. Within the bundle, we define a field data by invoking cloneType on the parameter. However, when we use a constructor parameter, this parameter becomes a public field of the class. When Chisel needs to clone the type of the Bundle, e.g., when it is used in a Vec, this public field is in the way. A solution (workaround) to this issue is to make the parameter field private:

```scala
class Port[T <: Data](private val dt: T) extends Bundle {
  val address = UInt(8.W)
  val data = dt.cloneType
}
```

With that new `Bundle`, we can define our router ports

```scala
class NocRouter2[T <: Data](dt: T, n: Int) extends Module {
  val io =IO(new Bundle {
    val inPort = Input(Vec(n, dt))
    val outPort = Output(Vec(n, dt))
  })

  // Route the payload according to the address
  // ...
```

and instantiate that router with a `Port` that takes a `Payload` as a parameter:

```scala
val router = Module(new NocRouter2(new Port(new Payload), 2))
```

9.2 Generate Combinational Logic

In Chisel, we can easily generate logic by creating a logic table with a Chisel `Vec` from a Scala `Array`. We might have data in a file, that we can read in during hardware generation time for the logic table. Listing 9.1 shows how to use the Scala `Source` class form the Scala standard library to read the file "data.txt", which contains integer constants in a textual representation.

A few words on the maybe a bit intimidating expression:

```scala
val table = VecInit(array.map(_.U(8.W)))
```

A Scala `Array` can be implicitly converted to a sequence (`Seq`), which supports the mapping function `map`. `map` invokes a function on each element of the sequence and returns a sequence of the return value of the function. Our function `_.U(8.W)` represents each `Int` value from the Scala array as a `_` and performs the conversion from a Scala `Int` value to a Chisel `UInt` literal, with a size of 8-bits. The Chisel object `VecInit` creates a Chisel `Vec` from a sequence `Seq` of Chisel types.

We can use the full power of Scala to generate our logic (tables). E.g., generate a table of fixpoint constants to represent a trigonometric function, compute constants for digital filters, or writing a small assembler in Scala to generate code for a microprocessor

```
import chisel3._
import scala.io.Source

class FileReader extends Module {
  val io = IO(new Bundle {
    val address = Input(UInt(8.W))
    val data = Output(UInt(8.W))
  })

  val array = new Array[Int](256)
  var idx = 0

  // read the data into a Scala array
  val source = Source.fromFile("data.txt")
  for (line <- source.getLines()) {
    array(idx) = line.toInt
    idx += 1
  }

  // convert the Scala integer array into the Chisel type Vec
  val table = VecInit(array.map(_.U(8.W)))

  // use the table
  io.data := table(io.address)
}
```

Listing 9.1: Reading a text file to generate a logic table.

9.2 GENERATE COMBINATIONAL LOGIC

```
import chisel3._

class BcdTable extends Module {
  val io = IO(new Bundle {
    val address = Input(UInt(8.W))
    val data = Output(UInt(8.W))
  })

  val array = new Array[Int](256)

  // Convert binary to BCD
  for (i <- 0 to 99) {
    array(i) = ((i/10)<<4) + i%10
  }

  val table = VecInit(array.map(_.U(8.W)))
  io.data := table(io.address)
}
```

Listing 9.2: Binary to binary-coded decimal conversion.

written in Chisel. All those functions are in the same code base (same language) and can be executed during hardware generation.

A classic example is the conversion of a binary number into a binary-coded decimal[1] (BCD) representation. BCD is used to represent a number in a decimal format using 4 bits fo each decimal digit. For example, decimal 13 is in binary 1101 and BCD encoded as 1 and 3 in binary: 00010011. BCD allows displaying numbers in decimal, a more user-friendly number representation than hexadecimal.

We can write a Java program that computes the table to convert binary to BCD. That Java program prints out VHDL code that can be included in a project. The Java program is about 100 lines of code; most of the code generating VHDL strings. The key part of the conversion is just two lines.

With Chisel, we can compute this table directly as part of the hardware generation. Listing 9.2 shows the table generation for the binary to BCD conversion.

---

[1] https://en.wikipedia.org/wiki/Binary-coded_decimal

87

9 Hardware Generators

```
class UpTicker(n: Int) extends Ticker(n) {
  val N = (n-1).U

  val cntReg = RegInit(0.U(8.W))

  cntReg := cntReg + 1.U
  when(cntReg === N) {
    cntReg := 0.U
  }

  io.tick := cntReg === N
}
```

Listing 9.3: Tick generation with a counter.

9.3 Use Inheritance

Chisel is an object-oriented language. A hardware component, the Chisel `Module` is a Scala class. Therefore, we can use inheritance to factor a common behavior out into a parent class. We explore how to use inheritance with an example.

In Section 6.2 we have explored different forms of counters, which may be used for a low-frequency tick generation. Let us assume we want to explore those different versions, e.g., to compare their resource requirement. We start with an abstract class to define the ticking interface:

```
abstract class Ticker(n: Int) extends Module {
  val io = IO(new Bundle{
    val tick = Output(Bool())
  })
}
```

Listing 9.3 shows a first implementation of that abstract class with a counter, counting up, for the tick generation.

We can test all different versions of our *ticker* logic with a single test bench. We *just* need to define the test bench to accept subtypes of `Ticker`. Listing 9.4 shows the Chisel code for the tester. The `TickerTester` has several parameters: (1) the type parameter [T <: Ticker] to accept a `Ticker` or any class that inherits from `Ticker`, (2) the design under test, being of type T or a subtype thereof, and (3) the number of clock cycles we expect for each tick. The tester waits for the first occurrence of a tick (the start might be different for different implementations) and then checks that tick repeats every *n* clock cycles.

With a first, easy implementation of the ticker, we can test the tester itself, probably with some println debugging. When we are confident that the simple ticker and the tester are correct, we can proceed and explore two more versions of the ticker. Listing 9.5 shows the tick generation with a counter counting down to 0. Listing 9.6 shows the nerd version of counting down to -1 to use less hardware by avoiding the comparator.

We can test all three versions of the ticker by using ScalaTest specifications, creating instances of the different versions of the ticker and passing them to the generic test bench. Listing 9.7 shows the specification. We run only the ticker tests with:

```
sbt "testOnly TickerSpec"
```

```
import chisel3.iotesters.PeekPokeTester
import org.scalatest._

class TickerTester[T <: Ticker](dut: T, n: Int) extends
    PeekPokeTester(dut: T) {

  // -1 is the notion that we have not yet seen the first tick
  var count = -1
  for (i <- 0 to n * 3) {
    if (count > 0) {
      expect(dut.io.tick, 0)
    }
    if (count == 0) {
      expect(dut.io.tick, 1)
    }
    val t = peek(dut.io.tick)
    // On a tick we reset the tester counter to N-1,
    // otherwise we decrement the tester counter
    if (t == 1) {
      count = n-1
    } else {
      count -= 1
    }

    step(1)
  }
}
```

Listing 9.4: A tester for different versions of the ticker.

9.3 USE INHERITANCE

```
class DownTicker(n: Int) extends Ticker(n) {

  val N = (n-1).U

  val cntReg = RegInit(N)

  cntReg := cntReg - 1.U
  when(cntReg === 0.U) {
    cntReg := N
  }

  io.tick := cntReg === N
}
```

Listing 9.5: Tick generation with a down counter.

```
class NerdTicker(n: Int) extends Ticker(n) {

  val N = n

  val MAX = (N - 2).S(8.W)
  val cntReg = RegInit(MAX)
  io.tick := false.B

  cntReg := cntReg - 1.S
  when(cntReg(7)) {
    cntReg := MAX
    io.tick := true.B
  }
}
```

Listing 9.6: Tick generation by counting down to -1.

```
class TickerSpec extends FlatSpec with Matchers {
  "UpTicker 5" should "pass" in {
    chisel3.iotesters.Driver(() => new UpTicker(5)) { c =>
      new TickerTester(c, 5)
    } should be (true)
  }

  "DownTicker 7" should "pass" in {
    chisel3.iotesters.Driver(() => new DownTicker(7)) { c =>
      new TickerTester(c, 7)
    } should be (true)
  }

  "NerdTicker 11" should "pass" in {
    chisel3.iotesters.Driver(() => new NerdTicker(11)) { c =>
      new TickerTester(c, 11)
    } should be (true)
  }
}
```

Listing 9.7: ScalaTest specifications for the ticker tests.

10 Example Designs

In this section, we explore some small size digital designs, such as a FIFO buffer, which are used as building blocks for a larger design. As another example, we design a serial interface (also called UART), which itself may use the FIFO buffer.

10.1 FIFO Buffer

We can decouple a write (sender) and a reader (receiver) by a buffer between the writer and reader. A common buffer is a first-in, first-out (FIFO) buffer. Figure 10.1 shows a writer, the FIFO, and a reader. Data is put into the FIFO by the writer on din with an active write signal. Data is read from the the FIFO by the reader on dout with an active read signal.

A FIFO is initially empty, singled by the empty signal. Reading from an empty FIFO is usually undefined. When data is written and never read a FIFO will become full. Writing to a full FIFO is usually ignored and the data lost. In other words, the signals empty and full serve as handshake signals

Several different implementations of a FIFO are possible: E.g., using on-chip memory and read and write pointers or simply a chain of registers with a tiny state machine. For small buffers (up to tens of elements) a FIFO organized with individual registers connected into a chain of buffers is a simple implementation with a low resource requirement. The code of the bubble FIFO is available in the chisel-examples[1] reposi-

---

[1] https://github.com/schoeberl/chisel-examples

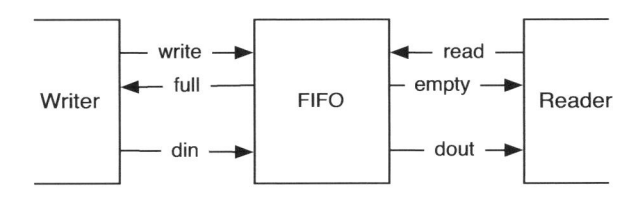

Figure 10.1: A writer, a FIFO buffer, and a reader.

tory.[2]

We start by defining the IO signals for the writer and the reader side. The size of the data is configurable with `size`. The write data are `din` and a write is signaled by `write`. The signal `full` performs the flow control[3] at the writer side.

```
class WriterIO(size: Int) extends Bundle {
  val write = Input(Bool())
  val full = Output(Bool())
  val din = Input(UInt(size.W))
}
```

The reader side provides data with `dout` and the read is initiated with `read`. The `empty` signal is responsible for the flow control at the reader side.

```
class ReaderIO(size: Int) extends Bundle {
  val read = Input(Bool())
  val empty = Output(Bool())
  val dout = Output(UInt(size.W))
}
```

Listing 10.1 shows a single buffer. The buffer has a enqueueing port `enq` of type `WriterIO` and a dequeueing port `deq` of type `ReaderIO`. The state elements of the buffer is one register that holds the data (`dataReg` and one state register for the simple FSM (`stateReg`). The FSM has only two states: either the buffer is `empty` or `full`. If the buffer is `empty`, a write will register the input data and change to the `full` state. If the buffer is `full`, a read will consume the data and change to the `empty` state. The IO ports `full` and `empty` represent the buffer state for the writer and the reader.

Listing 10.2 shows the complete FIFO. The complete FIFO has the same IO interface as the individual FIFO buffers. `BubbleFifo` has as parameters the `size` of the data word and `depth` for the number of buffer stages. We can build an `depth` stages bubble FIFO out of `depth` `FifoRegisters`. We crate the stages by filling them into a Scala `Array`. The Scala array has no hardware meaning, it *just* provides us with a container to have references to the created buffers. In a Scala `for` loop we connect the individual buffers. The first buffers enqueueing side is connected to the enqueueing IO of the complete FIFO and the last buffer's dequeueing side to the dequeueing side of the complete FIFO.

---

[2]For completeness, the Chisel book repository contains a copy of the FIFO code as well.
[3]https://en.wikipedia.org/wiki/Flow_control_(data)

10.1 FIFO Buffer

```
class FifoRegister(size: Int) extends Module {
  val io = IO(new Bundle {
    val enq = new WriterIO(size)
    val deq = new ReaderIO(size)
  })

  val empty :: full :: Nil = Enum(2)
  val stateReg = RegInit(empty)
  val dataReg = RegInit(0.U(size.W))

  when(stateReg === empty) {
    when(io.enq.write) {
      stateReg := full
      dataReg := io.enq.din
    }
  }.elsewhen(stateReg === full) {
    when(io.deq.read) {
      stateReg := empty
      dataReg := 0.U // just to better see empty slots in the
          waveform
    }
  }.otherwise {
    // There should not be an otherwise state
  }

  io.enq.full := (stateReg === full)
  io.deq.empty := (stateReg === empty)
  io.deq.dout := dataReg
}
```

Listing 10.1: A single stage of the bubble FIFO.

```
class BubbleFifo(size: Int, depth: Int) extends Module {
  val io = IO(new Bundle {
    val enq = new WriterIO(size)
    val deq = new ReaderIO(size)
  })

  val buffers = Array.fill(depth) { Module(new
      FifoRegister(size)) }
  for (i <- 0 until depth - 1) {
    buffers(i + 1).io.enq.din := buffers(i).io.deq.dout
    buffers(i + 1).io.enq.write := ~buffers(i).io.deq.empty
    buffers(i).io.deq.read := ~buffers(i + 1).io.enq.full
  }
  io.enq <> buffers(0).io.enq
  io.deq <> buffers(depth - 1).io.deq
}
```

Listing 10.2: A FIFO is composed of an array of FIFO bubble stages.

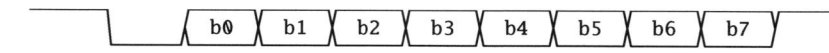

Figure 10.2: One byte transmitted by a UART.

10.2 A Serial Port

A serial port (also called UART[4] or RS-232[5]) is one of the easiest options to communicate between your laptop and an FPGA board. As the name implies, data is transmitted serially. An 8-bit byte is transmitted as follows: one start bit (0), the 8-bit data, least significant bit first, and then one or two stop bits (1). When no data is transmitted, the output is 1. Figure 10.2 shows the timing diagram of one byte transmitted.

We design our UART in a modular way with minimal functionality per module. We present a transmitter (TX), a receiver (RX), a buffer, and then usage of those base components.

First, we need an interface, a port definition. For the UART design, we use a ready/valid handshake interface, with the direction as seen from the transmitter.

---

[4]https://en.wikipedia.org/wiki/Universal_asynchronous_receiver-transmitter
[5]https://en.wikipedia.org/wiki/RS-232

10.2 A Serial Port

```
class Channel extends Bundle {
  val data = Input(Bits(8.W))
  val ready = Output(Bool())
  val valid = Input(Bool())
}
```

The convention of a ready/valid interface is that the data is transferred when both ready and valid are asserted.

Listing 10.3 shows a bare-bone serial transmitter (Tx). The IO ports are the txd port, where the serial data is sent and a Channel where the transmitter can receive the characters to serialize and send. To generate the correct timing, we compute a constant for by computing the time in clock cycles for one serial bit.

We use three registers: (1) register to shift the data (serialize them) (shiftReg), (2) a counter to generate the correct baud rate (cntReg), and (3) a counter for the number of bits that still need to be shifted out. No additional state register of FSM is needed, all state is encoded in those three registers.

Counter cntReg is continuously running (counting down to 0 and reset to the start value when 0). All action is only done when cntReg is 0. As we build a minimal transmitter, we have only the shift register to store the data. Therefore, the channel is only ready when cntReg is 0 and no bits are left to shift out.

The IO port txd is directly connected to the least significant bit of the shift register.

When there are more bits to shift out (bitsReg =/= 0.U), we shift the bits to the right and fill with 1 from the top (the idle level of a transmitter). If no more bits need to be shifted out, we check if the channel contains data (signaled with the valid port). If so, the bit string to be shifted out is constructed with one start bit (0), the 8-bit data, and two stop bits (1). Therefore, the bit count is set to 11.

This very minimal transmitter has no additional buffer and can accept a new character only when the shift register is empty and at the clock cycle when cntReg is 0. Accepting new data only when cntReg is 0 also means that the ready flag is also de-asserted when there would be space in the shift register. However, we do not want to add this "complexity" to the transmitter but delegate it to a buffer.

Listing 10.4 shows a single byte buffer, similar to the FIFO register for the bubble FIFO. The input port is a Channel interface, and the output is the Channel interface with flipped directions. The buffer contains the minimal state machine to indicate empty or full. The buffer driven handshake signals (in.ready and out.valid depend on the state register.

When the state is empty, and data on the input is valid, we register the data and switch to state full. When the state is full, and the downstream receiver is ready, the downstream data transfer happens, and we switch back to state empty.

```
class Tx(frequency: Int, baudRate: Int) extends Module {
  val io = IO(new Bundle {
    val txd = Output(Bits(1.W))
    val channel = new Channel()
  })

  val BIT_CNT = ((frequency + baudRate / 2) / baudRate -
      1).asUInt()

  val shiftReg = RegInit(0x7ff.U)
  val cntReg = RegInit(0.U(20.W))
  val bitsReg = RegInit(0.U(4.W))

  io.channel.ready := (cntReg === 0.U) && (bitsReg === 0.U)
  io.txd := shiftReg(0)

  when(cntReg === 0.U) {

    cntReg := BIT_CNT
    when(bitsReg =/= 0.U) {
      val shift = shiftReg >> 1
      shiftReg := Cat(1.U, shift(9, 0))
      bitsReg := bitsReg - 1.U
    }.otherwise {
      when(io.channel.valid) {
        // two stop bits, data, one start bit
        shiftReg := Cat(Cat(3.U, io.channel.data), 0.U)
        bitsReg := 11.U
      }.otherwise {
        shiftReg := 0x7ff.U
      }
    }

  }.otherwise {
    cntReg := cntReg - 1.U
  }
}
```

Listing 10.3: A transmitter for a serial port.

```
class Buffer extends Module {
  val io = IO(new Bundle {
    val in = new Channel()
    val out = Flipped(new Channel())
  })

  val empty :: full :: Nil = Enum(2)
  val stateReg = RegInit(empty)
  val dataReg = RegInit(0.U(8.W))

  io.in.ready := stateReg === empty
  io.out.valid := stateReg === full

  when(stateReg === empty) {
    when(io.in.valid) {
      dataReg := io.in.data
      stateReg := full
    }
  }.otherwise { // full
    when(io.out.ready) {
      stateReg := empty
    }
  }
  io.out.data := dataReg
}
```

Listing 10.4: A single-byte buffer with a ready/valid interface.

10 Example Designs

```
class BufferedTx(frequency: Int, baudRate: Int) extends Module {
  val io = IO(new Bundle {
    val txd = Output(Bits(1.W))
    val channel = new Channel()
  })
  val tx = Module(new Tx(frequency, baudRate))
  val buf = Module(new Buffer())

  buf.io.in <> io.channel
  tx.io.channel <> buf.io.out
  io.txd <> tx.io.txd
}
```

Listing 10.5: A transmitter with an additional buffer.

With that buffer we can extend our bare-bone transmitter. Listing 10.5 shows the combination of the transmitter `Tx` with a single-buffer in front. This buffer now relaxes the issue that `Tx` was `ready` only for single clock cycles. We delegated the solution of this issue to the buffer module. An extension of the single word buffer to a real FIFO can easily be done and needs no change in the transmitter or the single byte buffer.

Listing 10.6 shows the code for the receiver (`Rx`). A receiver is a little bit tricky, as it needs to reconstruct the timing of the serial data. The receiver waits for the falling edge of the start bit. From that event, the receiver waits 1.5 bit times to position itself into the middle of bit 0. Then it shifts in the bits every bit time. You can observe these two waiting times as `START_CNT` and `BIT_CNT`. For both times, the same counter (`cntReg`) is used. After 8 bits are shifted in, `valReg` signals an available byte

Listing 10.7 shows the usage of the serial port transmitter by sending a friendly message out. We define the message in a Scala string (`msg`) and converting it to a Chisel `Vec` of `UInt`. A Scala string is a sequence that supports the `map` method. The `map` method takes as argument a function literal, applies this function to each element, and builds a sequence of the functions return values. If the function literal shall have only one argument, as it is in this case, the argument can be represented by `_`. Our function literal calls the Chisel method `.U` to convert the Scala `Char` to a Chisel `UInt`. The sequence is then passed to `VecInint` to construct a Chisel `Vec`. We index into the vector `text` with the counter `cntReg` to provide the individual characters to the buffered transmitter. With each `ready` signal we increase the counter until the full string is sent out. The sender keeps `valid` asserted until the last character has been sent out.

Listing 10.8 shows the usage of the receiver and the transmitter by connecting them

10.2 A Serial Port

```scala
class Rx(frequency: Int, baudRate: Int) extends Module {
  val io = IO(new Bundle {
    val rxd = Input(Bits(1.W))
    val channel = Flipped(new Channel())
  })

  val BIT_CNT = ((frequency + baudRate / 2) / baudRate - 1).U
  val START_CNT = ((3 * frequency / 2 + baudRate / 2) /
      baudRate - 1).U

  // Sync in the asynchronous RX data
  val rxReg = RegNext(RegNext(io.rxd))

  val shiftReg = RegInit('A'.U(8.W))
  val cntReg = RegInit(0.U(20.W))
  val bitsReg = RegInit(0.U(4.W))
  val valReg = RegInit(false.B)

  when(cntReg =/= 0.U) {
    cntReg := cntReg - 1.U
  }.elsewhen(bitsReg =/= 0.U) {
    cntReg := BIT_CNT
    shiftReg := Cat(rxReg, shiftReg >> 1)
    bitsReg := bitsReg - 1.U
    // the last shifted in
    when(bitsReg === 1.U) {
      valReg := true.B
    }
  // wait 1.5 bits after falling edge of start
  }.elsewhen(rxReg === 0.U) {
    cntReg := START_CNT
    bitsReg := 8.U
  }

  when(valReg && io.channel.ready) {
    valReg := false.B
  }

  io.channel.data := shiftReg
  io.channel.valid := valReg
}
```

Listing 10.6: A receiver for a serial port.

10 Example Designs

```
class Sender(frequency: Int, baudRate: Int) extends Module {
  val io = IO(new Bundle {
    val txd = Output(Bits(1.W))
  })

  val tx = Module(new BufferedTx(frequency, baudRate))

  io.txd := tx.io.txd

  val msg = "Hello World!"
  val text = VecInit(msg.map(_.U))
  val len = msg.length.U

  val cntReg = RegInit(0.U(8.W))

  tx.io.channel.data := text(cntReg)
  tx.io.channel.valid := cntReg =/= len

  when(tx.io.channel.ready && cntReg =/= len) {
    cntReg := cntReg + 1.U
  }
}
```
Listing 10.7: Sending "Hello World!" via the serial port.

```
class Echo(frequency: Int, baudRate: Int) extends Module {
  val io = IO(new Bundle {
    val txd = Output(Bits(1.W))
    val rxd = Input(Bits(1.W))
  })

  val tx = Module(new BufferedTx(frequency, baudRate))
  val rx = Module(new Rx(frequency, baudRate))
  io.txd := tx.io.txd
  rx.io.rxd := io.rxd
  tx.io.channel <> rx.io.channel
}
```
Listing 10.8: Echoing data on the serial port.

together. This connection generates an Echo circuit where each received character is sent back (echoed).

10.3 Exercises

This exercise section is a little bit longer as it contains two exercises: (1) exploring the bubble FIFO and implement a different FIFO design; and (2) exploring the UART and extending it. Source code for both exercises is included in the chisel-examples[6] repository.

10.3.1 Explore FIFO Variations

The FIFO source also includes a tester that provokes different read and write behavior and generates a waveform in the value change dump (VCD)[7] format. The VCD file can be viewed with a waveform viewer, such as GTKWave[8]. Explore the FifoTester[9] in the repository. The repository contains a Makefile to run the examples, for the FIFO example just type:

```
$ make fifo
```

This make command will compile the FIFO, run the test, and starts GTKWave for waveform viewing. Explore the tester and the generated waveform.

In the first cycles, the tester writes a single word. We can observe in the waveform how that word bubbles through the FIFO, therefore the name *bubble FIFO*. This bubbling also means that the latency of a data word through the FIFO is equal to the depth of the FIFO.

The next test fills the FIFO until it is full. A single read follows. Notice how the empty word bubbles from the reader side of the FIFO to the writer side. When a bubble FIFO is full, it takes a latency of the buffer depth for a read to affect the writer side.

The end of the test contains a loop that tries to write and read at maximum speed. We can see the bubble FIFO running at maximum bandwidth, which is two clock cycles per word. A buffer stage has always to toggle between empty and full for a single word transfer.

---

[6]https://github.com/schoeberl/chisel-examples
[7]https://en.wikipedia.org/wiki/Value_change_dump
[8]http://gtkwave.sourceforge.net/
[9]https://github.com/schoeberl/chisel-examples/blob/master/src/test/scala/simple/FifoTester.scala

A bubble FIFO is simple and for small buffers has a low resource requirement. The main drawbacks of an n stage bubble FIFO are: (1) maximum throughput is one word every two clock cycles, (2) a data word has to travel n clock cycles from the writer end to the reader end, and (3) a full FIFO needs n clock cycles for the restart.

These drawbacks can be solved by a FIFO implementation with a circular buffer[10]. The circular buffer can be implemented with a memory and read and write pointers. Implement a FIFO as a circular buffer with four elements, using the same interface, and explore the different behavior with the tester. For an initial implementation of the circular buffer use, as a shortcut, a vector of registers (Reg(Vec(4, UInt(size.W)))).

10.3.2 The UART

For the UART example, you need an FPGA board with a serial port and a serial port for your laptop (usually with a USB connection). Connect the serial cable between the FPGA board and the serial port on your laptop. Start a terminal program, e.g., Hyperterm on Windows or gtkterm on Linux:

```
$ gtkterm &
```

Configure your port to use the correct device, with a USB UART this is often something like /dev/ttyUSB0. Set the baud rate to 115200 and no parity or flow control (handshake). With the following command you can create the Verilog code for the UART:

```
$ make uart
```

Then use your synthesize tool to synthesize the design. The repository contains a Quartus project for the DE2-115 FPGA board. With Quartus use the play button to synthesize the design and then configure the FPGA. After configuration, you should see a greeting message in the terminal.

Extend the blinking LED example with a UART and write 0 and 1 to the serial line when the LED is off and on. Use the BufferedTx, as in the Sender example.

With the slow output of characters (two per second), you can write the data to the UART transmit register and can ignore the read/valid handshake. Extend the example by writing repeated numbers 0-9 as fast as the baud rate allows. In this case, you have to extend your state machine to poll the UART status to check if the transmit buffer is free.

The example code contains only a single buffer for the Tx. Feel free to add the FIFO that you have implemented to add buffering to the transmitter and receiver.

---

[10]https://en.wikipedia.org/wiki/Circular_buffer

11 Design of a Processor

As one of the last chapters in this book, we present a medium size project: the design, simulation, and testing of a microprocessor. To keep this project manageable, we design a simple accumulator machine. The processor is called Leros[1] [8] and is available in open source at https://github.com/leros-dev/leros. We would like to mention that this is an advanced example and some computer architecture knowledge is needed to follow the presented code examples.

Leros is designed to be simple, but still a good target for a C compiler. The description of the instructions fits on one page, see Table 11.1. In that table A represents the accumulator, PC is the program counter, i is an immediate value (0 to 255), Rn a register n (0 to 255), o a branch offset relative to the PC, and AR an address register for memory access.

11.1 Start with an ALU

A central component of a processor is the arithmetic logic unit[2], or ALU for short. Therefore, we start with the coding of the ALU and a test bench. First, we define an Enum to represent the different operations of the ALU:

```
object Types {
  val nop :: add :: sub :: and :: or :: xor :: ld :: shr :: Nil
    = Enum(8)
}
```

An ALU usually has two operand inputs (call them a and b), an operation op (or opcode) input to select the function and an output y. Listing 11.1 shows the ALU.

We first define shorter names for the three inputs. The switch statement defines the logic for the computation of res. Therefore, it gets a default assignment of 0. The switch statement enumerates all operations and assigns the expression accordingly. All operations map directly to a Chisel expression. In the end, we assign the result res to the ALU output y

---
[1] https://leros-dev.github.io/
[2] https://en.wikipedia.org/wiki/Arithmetic_logic_unit

Opcode	Function	Description
add	A = A + Rn	Add register Rn to A
addi	A = A + i	Add immediate value i to A
sub	A = A - Rn	Subtract register Rn from A
subi	A = A - i	Subtract immediate value i from A
shr	A = A >>> 1	Shift A logically right
load	A = Rn	Load register Rn into A
loadi	A = i	Load immediate value i into A
and	A = A and Rn	And register Rn with A
andi	A = A and i	And immediate value i with A
or	A = A or Rn	Or register Rn with A
ori	A = A or i	Or immediate value i with A
xor	A = A xor Rn	Xor register Rn with A
xori	A = A xor i	Xor immediate value i with A
loadhi	$A_{15-8} = i$	Load immediate into second byte
loadh2i	$A_{23-16} = i$	Load immediate into third byte
loadh3i	$A_{31-24} = i$	Load immediate into fourth byte
store	Rn = A	Store A into register Rn
jal	PC = A, Rn = PC + 2	Jump to A and store return address in Rn
ldaddr	AR = A	Load address register AR with A
loadind	A = mem[AR+(i << 2)]	Load a word from memory into A
loadindbu	$A = mem[AR+i]_{7-0}$	Load a byte unsigned from memory into A
storeind	mem[AR+(i << 2)] = A	Store A into memory
storeindb	$mem[AR+i]_{7-0} = A$	Store a byte into memory
br	PC = PC + o	Branch
brz	if A == 0 PC = PC + o	Branch if A is zero
brnz	if A != 0 PC = PC + o	Branch if A is not zero
brp	if A >= 0 PC = PC + o	Branch if A is positive
brn	if A < 0 PC = PC + o	Branch if A is negative
scall	scall A	System call (simulation hook)

Table 11.1: Leros instruction set.

11.1 Start with an ALU

```
class Alu(size: Int) extends Module {
  val io = IO(new Bundle {
    val op = Input(UInt(3.W))
    val a = Input(SInt(size.W))
    val b = Input(SInt(size.W))
    val y = Output(SInt(size.W))
  })

  val op = io.op
  val a = io.a
  val b = io.b
  val res = WireInit(0.S(size.W))

  switch(op) {
    is(add) {
      res := a + b
    }
    is(sub) {
      res := a - b
    }
    is(and) {
      res := a & b
    }
    is(or) {
      res := a | b
    }
    is(xor) {
      res := a ^ b
    }
    is (shr) {
      // the following does NOT result in an unsigned shift
      // res := (a.asUInt >> 1).asSInt
      // work around
      res := (a >> 1) & 0x7fffffff.S
    }
    is(ld) {
      res := b
    }
  }

  io.y := res
}
```

Listing 11.1: The Leros ALU.

11 Design of a Processor

```scala
def alu(a: Int, b: Int, op: Int): Int = {
  op match {
    case 1 => a + b
    case 2 => a - b
    case 3 => a & b
    case 4 => a | b
    case 5 => a ^ b
    case 6 => b
    case 7 => a >>> 1
    case _ => -123 // This shall not happen
  }
}
```

Listing 11.2: The Leros ALU function written in Scala.

For the testing, we write the ALU function in plain Scala, as shown in Listing 11.2. While this duplication of hardware written in Chisel by a Scala implementation does not detect errors in the specification; it is at least some sanity check. We use some corner case values as the test vector:

```scala
// Some interesting corner cases
val interesting = Array(1, 2, 4, 123, 0, -1, -2, 0x80000000,
    0x7fffffff)
```

We test all functions with those values on both inputs:

```scala
def test(values: Seq[Int]) = {
  for (fun <- add to shr) {
    for (a <- values) {
      for (b <- values) {
        poke(dut.io.op, fun)
        poke(dut.io.a, a)
        poke(dut.io.b, b)
        step(1)
        expect(dut.io.y, alu(a, b, fun.toInt))
      }
    }
  }
}
```

Full, exhaustive testing for 32-bit arguments is not possible, which was the reason we selected some corner cases as input values. Beside testing against corner cases, it is also useful to test against random inputs:

```
val randArgs = Seq.fill(100)(scala.util.Random.nextInt)
test(randArgs)
```

You can run the tests within the Leros project with

```
$ sbt "test:runMain leros.AluTester"
```

and shall produce a success message similar to:

```
[info] [0.001] SEED 1544507337402
test Alu Success: 70567 tests passed in 70572 cycles taking
3.845715 seconds
[info] [3.825] RAN 70567 CYCLES PASSED
```

11.2 Decoding Instructions

From the ALU, we work backward and implement the instruction decoder. However, first, we define the instruction encoding in its own Scala class and a *shared* package. We want to share the encoding constants between the hardware implementation of Leros, an assembler for Leros, and an instruction set simulator of Leros.

```
package leros.shared {

object Constants {
  val NOP  = 0x00
  val ADD  = 0x08
  val ADDI = 0x09
  val SUB  = 0x0c
  val SUBI = 0x0d
  val SHR  = 0x10
  val LD   = 0x20
  val LDI  = 0x21
  val AND  = 0x22
  val ANDI = 0x23
  val OR   = 0x24
  val ORI  = 0x25
  val XOR  = 0x26
```

11 Design of a Processor

```
val XORI = 0x27
val LDHI = 0x29
val LDH2I = 0x2a
val LDH3I = 0x2b
val ST = 0x30
// ...
```

For the decode component, we define a Bundle for the output, which is later fed partially into the ALU.

```
class DecodeOut extends Bundle {
  val ena = Bool()
  val func = UInt()
  val exit = Bool()
}
```

Decode takes as input an 8-bit opcode and delivers the decoded signals as output. Those driving signals are assigned a default value with WireInit.

```
class Decode() extends Module {
  val io = IO(new Bundle {
    val din = Input(UInt(8.W))
    val dout = Output(new DecodeOut)
  })

  val f = WireInit(nop)
  val imm = WireInit(false.B)
  val ena = WireInit(false.B)

  io.dout.exit := false.B
```

The decoding itself is just a large switch statement on the part of the instruction that represents the opcode (in Leros for most instructions the upper 8 bits.)

```
  switch(io.din) {
    is(ADD.U) {
      f := add
      ena := true.B
    }
    is(ADDI.U) {
      f := add
      imm := true.B
      ena := true.B
```

110

```
}
is(SUB.U) {
  f   := sub
  ena := true.B
}
is(SUBI.U) {
  f   := sub
  imm := true.B
  ena := true.B
}
is(SHR.U) {
  f   := shr
  ena := true.B
}
// ...
```

11.3 Assembling Instructions

To write programs for Leros we need an assembler. However, for the very first test, we can hard code a few instructions, and put them into a Scala array, which we use to initialize the instruction memory.

```
val prog = Array[Int](
  0x0903, // addi 0x3
  0x09ff, // -1
  0x0d02, // subi 2
  0x21ab, // ldi 0xab
  0x230f, // and 0x0f
  0x25c3, // or 0xc3
  0x0000
)

def getProgramFix() = prog
```

However, this is a very inefficient approach to test a processor. Writing an assembler with an expressive language like Scala is not a big project. Therefore, we write a simple assembler for Leros, which is possible within about 100 lines of code. We define a function getProgram that calls the assembler. For branch destinations, we need a symbol table, which we collect in a Map. A classic assembler runs in two passes: (1) collect the values for the symbol table and (2) assemble the program with the symbols collected

11 Design of a Processor

in the first pass. Therefore, we call `assemble` twice with a parameter to indicate which pass it is.

```
def getProgram(prog: String) = {
  assemble(prog)
}

// collect destination addresses in first pass
val symbols = collection.mutable.Map[String, Int]()

def assemble(prog: String): Array[Int] = {
  assemble(prog, false)
  assemble(prog, true)
}
```

The `assemble` function starts with reading in the source file[3] and defining two helper functions to parse the two possible operands: (1) an integer constant (allowing decimal or hexadecimal notation) and (2) to read a register number.

```
def assemble(prog: String, pass2: Boolean): Array[Int] = {

  val source = Source.fromFile(prog)
  var program = List[Int]()
  var pc = 0

  def toInt(s: String): Int = {
    if (s.startsWith("0x")) {
      Integer.parseInt(s.substring(2), 16)
    } else {
      Integer.parseInt(s)
    }
  }

  def regNumber(s: String): Int = {
    assert(s.startsWith("r"), "Register numbers shall start
        with \'r\'")
    s.substring(1).toInt
  }
```

Listing 11.3 shows the core of the assembler for Leros. A Scala `match` expression

---

[3]This function does not actually read the source file, but for this discussion we can consider it as the reading function.

```
for (line <- source.getLines()) {
  if (!pass2) println(line)
  val tokens = line.trim.split(" ")
  val Pattern = "(.*:)".r
  val instr = tokens(0) match {
    case "//" => // comment
    case Pattern(l) => if (!pass2) symbols +=
        (l.substring(0, l.length - 1) -> pc)
    case "add" => (ADD << 8) + regNumber(tokens(1))
    case "sub" => (SUB << 8) + regNumber(tokens(1))
    case "and" => (AND << 8) + regNumber(tokens(1))
    case "or" => (OR << 8) + regNumber(tokens(1))
    case "xor" => (XOR << 8) + regNumber(tokens(1))
    case "load" => (LD << 8) + regNumber(tokens(1))
    case "addi" => (ADDI << 8) + toInt(tokens(1))
    case "subi" => (SUBI << 8) + toInt(tokens(1))
    case "andi" => (ANDI << 8) + toInt(tokens(1))
    case "ori" => (ORI << 8) + toInt(tokens(1))
    case "xori" => (XORI << 8) + toInt(tokens(1))
    case "shr" => (SHR << 8)
    // ...
    case "" => // println("Empty line")
    case t: String => throw new Exception("Assembler error: 
        unknown instruction: " + t)
    case _ => throw new Exception("Assembler error")
```

Listing 11.3: The main part of the Leros assembler.

covers the core of the assembly function.

11.4 Exercise

This exercise assignment in one of the last Chapters is in a very free form. You are at the end of your learning tour through Chisel and ready to tackle design problems that you find interesting.

One option is to reread the chapter and read along with all the source code in the Leros repository[4], run the test cases, fiddle with the code by breaking it and see that

---
[4] https://github.com/leros-dev/leros

tests fail.

Another option is to write your implementation of Leros. The implementation in the repository is just one possible organization of a pipeline. You could write a Chisel simulation version of Leros with just a single pipeline stage, or go creasy and superpipeline Leros for the highest possible clocking frequency.

A third option is to design your processor from scratch. Maybe the demonstration of how to build the Leros processor and the needed tools has convinced you that processor design and implementation is no magic art, but the engineering that can be very joyful.

12 Contributing to Chisel

Chisel is an open-source project under constant development and improvement. Therefore, you can also contribute to the project. Here we describe how to set up your environment for Chisel library development and how to contribute to Chisel.

12.1 Setup the Development Environment

Chisel consists of several different repositories; all hosted at the freechips organization at GitHub[1].

Fork the repository, which you like to contribute, into your personal GitHub account. You can fork the repository by pressing the Fork button in the GitHub web interface. Then from that fork, clone your fork of the repository. In our example, we change chisel3, and the clone command for my local fork is:

```
$ git clone git@github.com:schoeberl/chisel3.git
```

To compile Chisel 3 and publish as a local library execute:

```
$ cd chisel3
$ sbt compile
$ sbt publishLocal
```

Watch out during the publish local command for the version string of the published library, which contains the string SNAPSHOT. If you use the tester and the published version is not compatible with the Chisel SNAPSHOT, fork and clone the chisel-tester[2] repo as well and publish it locally.

To test your changes in Chisel, you probably also want to set up a Chisel project, e.g., by forking/cloning an empty Chisel project[3], renaming it, and removing the .git folder from it.

---

[1] https://github.com/freechipsproject
[2] https://github.com/freechipsproject/chisel-testers
[3] https://github.com/schoeberl/chisel-empty

12 CONTRIBUTING TO CHISEL

Change the `build.sbt` to reference the locally published version of Chisel. Furthermore, at the time of this writing, the head of Chisel source uses Scala 2.12, but Scala 2.12 has troubles with anonymous bundles[4]. Therefore, you need to add the following Scala option: `"-Xsource:2.11"`. The `build.sbt` should look similar to:

```
scalaVersion := "2.12.6"

scalacOptions := Seq("-Xsource:2.11")

resolvers ++= Seq(
  Resolver.sonatypeRepo("snapshots"),
  Resolver.sonatypeRepo("releases")
)

libraryDependencies +=
  "edu.berkeley.cs" %% "chisel3" % "3.2-SNAPSHOT"
libraryDependencies +=
  "edu.berkeley.cs" %% "chisel-iotesters" % "1.3-SNAPSHOT"
```

Compile your Chisel test application and take a close look if it picks up the local published version of the Chisel library (there is also a SNAPSHOT version published, so if, e.g., the Scala version is different between your Chisel library and your application code, it picks up the SNAPSHOT version from the server instead of your local published library.)

See also some notes at the Chisel repo[5].

12.2 Testing

When you change the Chisel library, you should run the Chisel tests. In an sbt based project, this is usually run with:

```
$ sbt test
```

Furthermore, if you add functionality to Chisel, you should also provide tests for the new features.

---

[4]https://github.com/freechipsproject/chisel-template/issues/35
[5]https://github.com/freechipsproject/chisel3#for-chisel-developers

12.3 Contribute with a Pull Request

In the Chisel project, no developer commits directly to the main repository. A contribution is organized via a pull request[6] from a branch in a forked version of the library. For further information, see the documentation at GitHub on collaboration with pull requests[7]. The Chisel group started to document contribution guidelines[8].

12.4 Exercise

Invent a new operator for the UInt type, implement it in the Chisel library, and write some usage/test code to explore the operator. It does not need to be a useful operator; just anything will be good, e.g., a ? operator that delivers the lefthand side if it is different from 0 otherwise the righthand side. Sounds like a multiplexer, right? How many lines of code did you need to add?[9]

As simple as this was, please be not tempted to fork the Chisel project and add your little extensions. Changes and extension shall be coordinated with the main developers. This exercise was just a simple exercise to get you started.

If you are getting bold, you could pick one of the open issues[10] and try to solve it. Then contribute with a pull request to Chisel. However, probably first watch the style of development in Chisel by watching the GitHub repositories. See how changes and pull requests are handled in the Chisel open-source project.

---

[6] https://help.github.com/articles/creating-a-pull-request-from-a-fork/
[7] https://help.github.com/categories/collaborating-with-issues-and-pull-requests/
[8] https://github.com/freechipsproject/chisel-lang-governance/blob/master/reviewer_guidelines.md
[9] A quick and dirty implementation needs just two lines of Scala code.
[10] https://github.com/freechipsproject/chisel3/issues

13 Summary

This book presented an introduction to digital design using the hardware construction language Chisel. We have seen several simple to medium-sized digital circuits described in Chisel. Chisel is embedded in Scala and therefore inherits the powerful abstraction of Scala. As this book is intended as an introduction, we have restricted our examples to simple uses of Scala. A next logical step is to learn a few basics of Scala and apply them to your Chisel project.

I would be happy to receive feedback on the book, as I will further improve it and will publish new editions. You can contact me at `mailto:masca@dtu.dk`, or with an issue request on the GitHub repository. I am also happily accepting pull requests for the book repository for any fixes and improvements.

Source Access

This book is available in open source. The repository also contains slides for a Chisel course and all Chisel examples: `https://github.com/schoeberl/chisel-book`

A collection of medium-sized examples, which most are referenced in the book, is also available in open source. This collection also contains projects for various popular FPGA boards: `https://github.com/schoeberl/chisel-examples`

A Chisel Projects

Chisel is not (yet) used in many projects. Therefore, open-source Chisel code to learn the language and the coding style is rare. Here we list several projects we are aware of that use Chisel and are in open source.

Rocket Chip[1] is a RISC-V[2] [13] processor-complex generator that comprises the Rocket microarchitecture and TileLink interconnect generators. Originally developed at UC Berkeley as the first chip-scale Chisel project [1], Rocket Chip is now commercially supported by SiFive[3].

Sodor[4] is a collection of RISC-V implementations intended for educational use. It contains 1, 2, 3, and 5 stages pipeline implementations. All processors use a simple scratchpad memory shared by instruction fetch, data access, and program loading via a debug port. Sodor is mainly intended to be used in simulation.

Patmos[5] is an implementation of a processor optimized for real-time systems [10]. The Patmos repository includes several multicore communication architectures, such as a time-predictable memory arbiter [7], a network-on-chip [9] a shared scratchpad memory with an ownership [11]. At the time of this writing, Patmos is still described in Chisel 2.

FlexPRET[6] is an implementation of a precision timed architecture [14]. FlexPRET implements the RISC-V instruction set and has been updated to Chisel 3.1.

Lipsi[7] is a tiny processor intended for utility functions on a system-on-chip [6]. As the code base of Lipsi is very small, it can serve as an easy starting point for processor design in Chisel. Lipsi also showcases the productivity of Chisel/Scala. It took me 14 hours to describe the hardware in Chisel and run it on an FPGA, write an assembler in Scala, write a Lipsi instruction set simulator in Scala for co-simulation, and write a few test cases in Lipsi assembler.

OpenSoC Fabric[8] is an open-source NoC generator written in Chisel [5]. It is intended to provide a system-on-chip for large-scale design exploration. The NoC itself is a

---
[2] https://en.wikipedia.org/wiki/RISC-V
[3] https://www.sifive.com/

A Chisel Projects

state-of-the-art design with wormhole routing, credits for flow control, and virtual channels. OpenSoC Fabric is still using Chisel 2.

RoCC[9] is a neural network accelerator that integrates with the RISC-V Rocket processor [4]. RoCC supports inference and learning.

If you know an open-source project that uses Chisel, please drop me a note so I can include it in a future edition of the book.

B Chisel 2

This book covers version 3 of Chisel. Moreover, Chisel 3 is recommended for new designs. However, there is still Chisel 2 code out in the wild, which has not yet been converted to Chisel 3. There is documentation available on how to convert a Chisel 2 project to Chisel 3:

- Chisel2 vs. Chisel3[1] and
- Towards Chisel 3[2]

However, you might get involved in a project that still uses Chisel 2, e.g., the Patmos[3] [10] processor. Therefore, we provide here some information on Chisel 2 coding for those who have started with Chisel 3.

First, all documentation on Chisel 2 has been removed from the web sites belonging to Chisel. We have rescued those PDF documents and put them on GitHub at https://github.com/schoeberl/chisel2-doc. You can use the Chisel 2 tutorial by switching to the Chisel 2 branch:

```
$ git clone https://github.com/ucb-bar/chisel-tutorial.git
$ cd chisel-tutorial
$ git checkout chisel2
```

The main visible difference between Chisel 3 and 2 are the definitions of constants, bundles for IO, wires, memories, and probably older forms of register definitions.

Chisel 2 constructs can be used, to some extent, in a Chisel 3 project by using the compatibility layer using as package Chisel instead of chisel3. However, using this compatibility layer should only be used in a transition phase. Therefore, we do not cover it here.

Here are two examples of basic components, the same that have been presented for Chisel 3. A module containing combinational logic:

---

[1] https://github.com/freechipsproject/chisel3/wiki/Chisel3-vs-Chisel2
[2] https://github.com/schoeberl/chisel-examples/blob/master/TowardsChisel3.md
[3] https://github.com/t-crest/patmos

B Chisel 2

```
import Chisel._

class Logic extends Module {
  val io = new Bundle {
    val a = UInt(INPUT, 1)
    val b = UInt(INPUT, 1)
    val c = UInt(INPUT, 1)
    val out = UInt(OUTPUT, 1)
  }

  io.out := io.a & io.b | io.c
}
```

Note that the `Bundle` for the IO definition is *not* wrapped into an `IO()` class. Furthermore, the direction of the different IO ports is defined as part of the type definition, in this example as `INPUT` and `OUTPUT` as part of `UInt`. The width is given as the second parameter.

The 8-bit register example in Chisel 2:

```
import Chisel._

class Register extends Module {
  val io = new Bundle {
    val in = UInt(INPUT, 8)
    val out = UInt(OUTPUT, 8)
  }

  val reg = Reg(init = UInt(0, 8))
  reg := io.in

  io.out := reg
}
```

Here you see a typical register definition with a reset value passed in as a `UInt` to the named parameter `init`. This form is still valid in Chisel 3, but the usage of `RegInit` and `RegNext` is recommended for new Chisel 3 designs. Note also here the constant definition of an 8-bit wide 0 as `UInt(0, 8)`.

Chisel based testing C++ code and Verilog code are generated by calling `chiselMainTest` and `chiselMain`. Both "main" functions take a `String` array for further parameters.

```
import Chisel._
```

```
class LogicTester(c: Logic) extends Tester(c) {
  poke(c.io.a, 1)
  poke(c.io.b, 0)
  poke(c.io.c, 1)
  step(1)
  expect(c.io.out, 1)
}
object LogicTester {
  def main(args: Array[String]): Unit = {
    chiselMainTest(Array("--genHarness", "--test",
      "--backend", "c",
      "--compile", "--targetDir", "generated"),
      () => Module(new Logic())) {
        c => new LogicTester(c)
      }
  }
}

import Chisel._

object LogicHardware {
  def main(args: Array[String]): Unit = {
    chiselMain(Array("--backend", "v"), () => Module(new
        Logic()))
  }
}
```

A memory with sequential registered read and write ports is defined in Chisel 2 as:

```
val mem = Mem(UInt(width = 8), 256, seqRead = true)
val rdData = mem(Reg(next = rdAddr))
when(wrEna) {
  mem(wrAddr) := wrData
}
```

Bibliography

[1] Krste Asanović, Rimas Avizienis, Jonathan Bachrach, Scott Beamer, David Biancolin, Christopher Celio, Henry Cook, Daniel Dabbelt, John Hauser, Adam Izraelevitz, Sagar Karandikar, Ben Keller, Donggyu Kim, John Koenig, Yunsup Lee, Eric Love, Martin Maas, Albert Magyar, Howard Mao, Miquel Moreto, Albert Ou, David A. Patterson, Brian Richards, Colin Schmidt, Stephen Twigg, Huy Vo, and Andrew Waterman. The rocket chip generator. Technical Report UCB/EECS-2016-17, EECS Department, University of California, Berkeley, Apr 2016.

[2] Jonathan Bachrach, Huy Vo, Brian Richards, Yunsup Lee, Andrew Waterman, Rimas Avizienis, John Wawrzynek, and Krste Asanovic. Chisel: constructing hardware in a Scala embedded language. In Patrick Groeneveld, Donatella Sciuto, and Soha Hassoun, editors, *The 49th Annual Design Automation Conference (DAC 2012)*, pages 1216–1225, San Francisco, CA, USA, June 2012. ACM.

[3] William J. Dally, R. Curtis Harting, and Tor M. Aamodt. *Digital design using VHDL: A systems approach*. Cambridge University Press, 2016.

[4] Schuyler Eldridge, Amos Waterland, Margo Seltzer, and Jonathan Appavooand Ajay Joshi. Towards general-purpose neural network computing. In *2015 International Conference on Parallel Architecture and Compilation (PACT)*, pages 99–112, Oct 2015.

[5] Farzaf Fatollahi-Fard, David Donofrio, George Michelogiannakis, and John Shalf. Opensoc fabric: On-chip network generator. In *2016 IEEE International Symposium on Performance Analysis of Systems and Software (ISPASS)*, pages 194–203, April 2016.

[6] Martin Schoeberl. Lipsi: Probably the smallest processor in the world. In *Architecture of Computing Systems – ARCS 2018*, pages 18–30. Springer International Publishing, 2018.

[7] Martin Schoeberl, David VH Chong, Wolfgang Puffitsch, and Jens Sparsø. A time-predictable memory network-on-chip. In *Proceedings of the 14th International*

Workshop on Worst-Case Execution Time Analysis (WCET 2014), pages 53–62, Madrid, Spain, July 2014.

[8] Martin Schoeberl and Morten Borup Petersen. Leros: The return of the accumulator machine. In Martin Schoeberl, Thilo Pionteck, Sascha Uhrig, Jürgen Brehm, and Christian Hochberger, editors, *Architecture of Computing Systems - ARCS 2019 - 32nd International Conference, Proceedings*, pages 115–127. Springer, 1 2019.

[9] Martin Schoeberl, Luca Pezzarossa, and Jens Sparsø. A minimal network interface for a simple network-on-chip. In Martin Schoeberl, Thilo Pionteck, Sascha Uhrig, Jürgen Brehm, and Christian Hochberger, editors, *Architecture of Computing Systems - ARCS 2019*, pages 295–307. Springer, 1 2019.

[10] Martin Schoeberl, Wolfgang Puffitsch, Stefan Hepp, Benedikt Huber, and Daniel Prokesch. Patmos: A time-predictable microprocessor. *Real-Time Systems*, 54(2):389–423, Apr 2018.

[11] Martin Schoeberl, Tórur Biskopstø Strøm, Oktay Baris, and Jens Sparsø. Scratchpad memories with ownership. In *2019 Design, Automation and Test in Europe Conference Exhibition (DATE)*, 2019.

[12] Bill Venners, Lex Spoon, and Martin Odersky. *Programming in Scala, 3rd Edition*. Artima Inc, 2016.

[13] Andrew Waterman, Yunsup Lee, David A. Patterson, and Krste Asanovic. The risc-v instruction set manual, volume i: Base user-level isa. Technical Report UCB/EECS-2011-62, EECS Department, University of California, Berkeley, May 2011.

[14] Michael Zimmer. *Predictable Processors for Mixed-Criticality Systems and Precision-Timed I/O*. PhD thesis, EECS Department, University of California, Berkeley, Aug 2015.

Printed in Great Britain
by Amazon